ACTOR NEEDS RESTRAINT!

ACTOR NEEDS RESTRAINT!

MONOLOGUES, RECITATIONS, CLOWN TURNS, AND COMEDY SKETCHES

Volume 1

ANDY JONES

Breakwater Books
P.O. Box 2188, St. John's, NL, Canada, A1C 6E6
www.breakwaterbooks.com

A CIP catalogue record for this book is available from Library and Archives Canada.

ISBN 9781550819793 (softcover)
© 2024 Andy Jones

All rights reserved. No part of this publication may be reproduced, stored in a retrieval system or transmitted, in any form or by any means, without the prior written consent of the publisher or a licence from The Canadian Copyright Licensing Agency (Access Copyright). For an Access Copyright licence, visit www.accesscopyright.ca or call toll free 1-800-893-5777.

We acknowledge the support of the Canada Council for the Arts. We acknowledge the financial support of the Government of Canada through the Department of Heritage and the Government of Newfoundland and Labrador through the Department of Tourism, Culture, Arts and Recreation for our publishing activities.

Printed and bound in India by Imprint Press.

Breakwater Books is committed to choosing papers and materials for our books that help to protect our environment. To this end, this book is printed on a recycled paper and other sources that are certified by the Forest Stewardship Council®.

For Mary-Lynn Bernard.
So glad you came back from Guyana.
Finally...

CONTENTS

Introduction **ix**
A Note from Andy Jones **xiii**

ALL HIS OLD MATERIAL IS...OUT OF THE BIN 1
KING O' FUN (A LEAP O' FAITH) 67
AN EVENING WITH UNCLE VAL 121

Acknowledgements **185**

INTRODUCTION

The three shows printed in this book are only a small part of the work of Andy Jones over his creative lifetime. They are all solo shows, written and performed by Andy, intended for the theatre. The first of them was performed in 1983, so a little context is perhaps in order.

In April of 1976, Sandra Gwyn wrote a piece in *Saturday Night* that heralded the revival of art and theatre in Newfoundland during the 1960s and 70s that she called a "renaissance." For those people making art and theatre at the time, it certainly felt like that, and as Andy tells us here in his show *An Evening with Uncle Val*, it was a heady time to be young and creative in Newfoundland—to be part of a theatre that was determined to tell its own stories, in its own dialect and to its own people.

Fifty years on, it is perhaps hard to imagine a time in which that was not the case, but so it was. The collective energy and anarchy of those days is fondly remembered by those who were there, as is the sense of mission to create, at the LSPU Hall, the National Theatre of Newfoundland (as I remember Andy saying). Indeed, always as part of that story is to be found the figure of Andy Jones, whether as a member of the great comedy company CODCO or a leader in the development of the Hall as a space for all. As filmmaker of the celebrated *The Adventure of Faustus Bidgood*, as advocate for the Jack stories, as Prospero in *The Newfoundland Tempest*, in his series of one-person shows, and in projects and plays too numerous to list, Andy was a vital part of the creative renaissance in Newfoundland that Gwyn wrote of.

The present generation of theatre makers in Newfoundland stands, as the Ode says, "where once they stood." And Andy remains relevant in the present day as a theatre maker, as his show *Don't Give Up on Me, Dad* this last summer proved. Indeed, an important part of what Andy and his one-person shows have done over the years is to give to younger Newfoundland theatre makers inspiring evidence that you can make a life doing theatre and that the country cares about stories from here. That we can be ourselves on stage and that it can be a lifelong activity and occupation. I also feel that while the title of this book is from a review suggesting Andy needed "Restraint," one of the many creative lessons we've all taken from his shows is an encouragement to let our minds and imaginations run wild.

When Andy is on stage, performing solo, he's accompanied by ghosts of Newfoundland's past. They gather with him, delighted to be remembered by and with him and, in their way, supporting him in the great loneliness of the solo performance.

In our town out here at the edge of Canada, he is an iconic and very familiar figure in the downtown. It is a very St. John's thing to run into Andy, often with a small dog, walking and working something out in his head, and then he will invariably take the time to ask about your life and how things are. He's known for his reflective jacket and wool hat in the winter, and longer shorts, T-shirt, open button-down shirt and dog in summer. The Artist in his Community, known and respected.

The words in this book are only a part of his contribution to the place. Of course, his life partner, Mary-Lynn, is equally important and recognized, a community builder in her own right, and was, has been, and will be instrumental in ways no one can either imagine or understand in bringing Andy's shows to the stage. Indeed, Mary-Lynn had a big part in causing *Out of the Bin* to be produced and performed.

In 1983 I was living out in Topsail, twenty-eight years old, in what amounted to a shack, trying to work out what to do with myself, banged up by a spectacular theatre accident in Toronto. I can remember collecting bottles from the side of the road to trade in for milk, single cigarettes and newspapers, listening to CBC all day, inching towards the notion of going back to school and doing an MA in history at MUN and giving up on whatever life I'd lived up until then.

Then a knock came to the door, and there was Andy, come to ask me to help him get a show together as a fundraiser to help send Mary-Lynn to Guyana as part of Canadian Crossroads International.

That show became *Out of the Bin*, one of the works you are holding in your hand right now. I have come to realize while preparing this introduction that my life would have been very different without that knock on the door. Since then, Andy and I have collaborated on three other solo shows of his: *King o' Fun, To the Wall*, and, just this past year, *Don't Give Up on Me, Dad*. I wrote my letter to apply for a life-changing job at the University of Alberta drama department in his kitchen in Toronto one Christmas; we joined Equity together by accident when working on *Pope Joan* at Nightwood Theatre; he encouraged me to be Artistic Animateur at the Hall and introduced me to Martha Henry; we have been to the Yukon, Tasmania, Glasgow, and points in between. In short, for me, as for all my contemporaries in St. John's theatre, Andy has been a constant throughout my creative life, even when we weren't living in the same province.

Whether in Newfoundland, Toronto, London, or Alberta, I can hear his voice in my memory, see us both in rehearsals, sometimes lying on the floor, telling stories and always asking what is the very essence and nature of narrative, the anatomy of story.

Since *Out of the Bin*, audiences have come to know what to expect from an Andy Jones show; they have faith in him and what they will get from him. That is an artistic contract of trust that many of us in the theatre aspire to but very rarely achieve, especially over a career and creative life spanning fifty years. Somewhere at the bottom of all this has been the way that Andy's artistic and personal priorities have always been ahead of any notion of success.

He remains, in his mid-70s, relevant and adaptable. He is still our theatre's greatest advocate, mentor, cheerleader, and talent scout. Theatre practice has greatly changed over our creative lives, and Andy has always managed to find ways to adapt, to change his focus, while remaining true to himself. His wonderful Jack stories, now published and beautifully illustrated by new collaborators, have earned him a wider audience; his work with puppets and his continuing generosity with his time as a senior theatre practitioner in his community are just a few of the ways he has changed, developed, and adapted.

The shows in this book can be taken many different ways, and I know Andy hopes that other performers might find some of the scenes, sketches, or ideas in these pages appealing enough to rehearse and perform them—perhaps to attempt their own version of the "Giant Budgie." The shows can be read in order or browsed through, depending on what strikes one's fancy; "All of Chekhov in a Few Pages" one day, the "Rooster Bishop of Borino" on another.

I think it was while working on *To the Wall* that the notion first came to me that these solo shows were, among other things, all honest love letters to Newfoundland, to the idea of the place and the people, to the history and landscape, language and culture. These shows chart a long creative relationship and love affair with this place that has only deepened with the passage of time and as Andy's skill and strength as a solo performer have grown and developed.

So, as the songs say, to end and conclude…this past summer, Andy performed his latest work, *Don't Give Up on Me, Dad*, and the opening-night audience was filled with people, many of whom had flown home especially for the occasion. It was important to them that they were on hand to support Andy in the work, and by their presence to both acknowledge his support of them in the past and demonstrate their love for him. To thank him for his lifelong generosity with his time and attention. He is well-known for his attendance at other people's shows and for always having a considered and thoughtful response when asked about what he has seen. He always gives you something.

Our Andy.

Charlie Tomlinson
St. John's, December 2023

A NOTE FROM ANDY JONES

I have been writing and performing comedy sketches, monologues, stand-up routines, and funny bits for over fifty years. These short forms are my beat—my default form of expression. The three plays in this book are collections of these short pieces—with some haphazard connecting material in between.

No doubt I went down this path because of a misspent youth listening to *The Goon Show* on radio, memorizing the British music-hall monologues of Stanley Holloway and every comedy sketch in *Beyond the Fringe*. I always performed in the school oratorical contests where we recited the poems of Robert Service, Henry Wadsworth Longfellow, and Alfred Noyes; the soliloquies of William Shakespeare; and that perennial favourite: Lincoln's Gettysburg Address. I listened attentively to and mocked the beautifully constructed and frightening sermons of the Catholic priests. And of course, I eagerly listened to a million well-crafted stories from my very funny Mom and Dad. Oh, and Dad had a tape recorder! A rare thing in those days. My friends—including the brilliant young Greg Malone—and I spent too many hours recording our sketches, characters, and imitations of teachers and famous people.

Years later, one of my first professional jobs was as an actor in a year-long European tour of British sketch comedy writer Ken Campbell's *Pilk's Madhouse*. This was followed by seven years with the CODCO sketch comedy troupe in both its theatre and TV incarnations. I wrote and performed many monologues during those years—including the letters of Uncle Val, the sermons of Father Dinn and Reverend Freep, and the ravings of Ricardo Huerta.

I think some of these sketches really hit the mark. I'm proud of those. With others I had to squeeze the laughs out. But to maintain the integrity of the plays I have included them all.

In light of our evolved modern sensibilities, some of my language may seem insensitive. I apologize for that—though I often left it in—I want these scripts to be something of a record of the times in which they were written. Future performers may remove those parts.

I had fun doing these shows. I hope you have fun reading and performing them.

Andy Jones
St. John's, February 2024

"ALL HIS OLD MATERIAL IS OUT OF THE BIN"

A BENEFIT SHOW FOR

ANDY JONES AND CANADIAN CROSSROADS INTERNATIONAL

ANDY JONES PERFORMS HIS GREATEST HITS

DIRECTED BY
CHARLES TOMLINSON

CO-PRODUCED BY
ANDY JONES
AND
RESOURCE CENTRE FOR THE ARTS

FRIDAY & SATURDAY... JUNE 17 & 18
8:30 P.M.

LSPU HALL, VICTORIA ST.

ADMISSION $3.00

POSTER: NICE GUY GRAPHICS

ALL HIS OLD MATERIAL IS...
OUT OF THE BIN
by Andy Jones

With additional material by the Sheila's Brush Theatre Company, including their adaptation of the folktale "Jack Ships to a Cat," as told by Mr. Pius Power Sr. of Clattice Harbour Southwest—and a few words by William Shakespeare.

TABLE OF CONTENTS

A catalogue of the several monologues, comedy bits, one-man sketches, and passionate ravings contained in *Out of the Bin*, which an actor performs in and near his own bed as he melodramatically laments his loneliness, artistic failings, and career shortcomings.

Part One

Comedian Takes to His Bed 4
A Nail up My Nose...10
Oil for America, Part One: Moving Newfoundland to Arizona 12
Why Is That Funny? A Lecture on Comedy
    (with Personal Confessions) 14
No Man Is an Actor: The Arts in Newfoundland, 1983.......................... 17

The Shitting Pig: A Special Talent 21
The Soft-Spot Murderer 23
Infuriating Humour 25
Ricardo's Origin Story, Part One: Pit of Vipers 28
The Irish Factor: Father Dinn on St. Patrick 32
Tales of Meanness: Reverend Freep's Christmas Message 33
Bayman in Exile: Uncle Val on St. John's 35
Catholic Jokes: Father Dinn on Sin 36

Part Two

The Audience in My Bedroom 40
"Such Stuff As Dreams Are Made On," by Will Shakespeare 41
Jack Meets the Cat: Episode One 42
Ricardo's Origin Story, Part Two: Mom, Pop, and Fiery Red Wine 43
TENSE UP! (1983 National Theatre School Training) 45
Oil for America, Part Two: Wake Up, Canada! America Is Inside You 46
News for Stupid People 48
Frozen Stiff and Shrivelled: Spring in Newfoundland 49
Oil for America, Part Three: We're Comin' to Get Ya, Peckford! 51
"Nob Gobbling": Obscenity on the Stage 52
Ménage à Sept 54
Jack Meets the Cat: Episode Two 56
Hello, Shackles! Hello Chains!—Father Dinn on Marriage 60
Tin Bed Bends; Story Ends 61

ANDY JONES'S NOTES ON *OUT OF THE BIN*

This show is a collection of bits, sketches, monologues, and clown turns that I wrote and performed during my first eleven years as an actor/ writer. I drew them all together by having me, a thirty-five-year-old depressed actor—totally alone—in bed, in my room, despairing about my career. My only friends were the comedy characters I had created.

I had previously performed some of these short pieces on the radio, in the CODCO sketch comedy theatre troupe, or with the Sheila's Brush

Theatre Company. Others I'd done for my family in the living room when I was a kid.

I put this show together in June 1983 as a benefit—ticket price $3.00—for Mary-Lynn Bernard's Crossroads International trip to Guyana.

Some of the material deals softly with the issues of the times. It was the early 1980s, and the discovery of offshore oil was leading to big questions in Newfoundland and Labrador; the influence of the Catholic church was of course always at the top of my mind, as were the daily melodramas of the struggling artist. But the show was mostly fun bits.

In *Out of the Bin* I was going for a relaxed and personal tone that I had never seen in the theatre before. When I wasn't in the middle of a sketch, I was determined to speak to the audience as if they were a close friend who had chanced upon me working out some ideas for a show while at the same time wallowing in arts-related self-pity. Somehow it got laughs—honestly.

The critics loved it or hated it. It was called "a shaggy shapeless series of sketches," which I mostly agree with. I was called an amiable raconteur/slob. I was told that I needed restraint—hence the title of this book. I was young. I guess I was trying to be gross, to shock, to see how far I could go, so I proudly did the Shitting Pig, the Soft-Spot Murderer, the vomiting instructions, the green fog burps, Father Dinn's dick, etc. It all seems very puny now, compared to the later comedy of *South Park* or Sacha Baron Cohen.

I also loved to walk the tightrope of "not funny" funny—especially in my "Lecture on Comedy." That's dangerous territory, and it was quite edgy for those times—I hate to say it, but I guess you had to be there...

One critic said "it was a revolting play" that hid my "real talent." I'm not sure I agree with the "real talent" part. But somehow, I pulled this show out of the waste bin—and got a few life-affirming laughs.

And—if you're interested in performing any of these pieces—by all means try your luck!

—AJ, December 2023

PART ONE

The time: Spring 1983

The setting: The unbelievably messy bedroom of a person who has not been out of bed for six months. No cleaning has taken place during that time. Newspapers, magazines, takeout cups, pizza boxes, chip bags, and dirty socks are piled deep.

Things have, however, not been thrown around the room. They have been piled on top of each other over a long period of despair.

ANDY lies under the covers of his bed at stage right centre. He is wearing a striped pyjama top. There is a bedside table to the right of the bed on which there is an open box of chocolates, a roll of toilet paper, a hammer, a sticky bun, and other stale foodstuffs. On the floor under the table are a small tub of margarine and a tiny toy drum and drumsticks. Between this table and the bed, facing the audience, there is a chair—on which sit a clock radio and an electric kettle. To ANDY's left is another chair, with a candle on it.

A small table and chair have been placed stage left. On the table there are papers and pens and a small cassette tape recorder, a few cassettes, a flashlight and index cards, which are laid out in piles. Extreme stage left there is a large outdoor metal garbage bin.

COMEDIAN TAKES TO HIS BED

As the lights come up, ANDY is lying in bed, looking off into space for an incredibly long time. Keeps looking. It's getting to be an uncomfortably long time now. Still looking. More time passes. He's prostrate with depression and arts-related despair. Then his head falls to one side. This is the first sign of movement.

ANDY: Oh, my Jeezez. *(These words barely escape his lips. He stays for a long time in this new head position.)* Oh my. Oh…Oh…Oh…Oh…Oh. *(These words also barely escape his lips. Eventually his right hand comes up, almost corpselike, barely able to move. It stops in mid-air. Then it reaches out and goes to the box of chocolates—in a surprisingly nimble finger search, the hand locates just the right chocolate. ANDY drops the chocolate into his mouth.)*

ANDY: *(He moans theatrically through the chocolate munching.)* Oh, my Jeezez. Oh…Oh. Oh. Oh. Oh…Umm, oh. Oh, my Jeezez. *(Pause. ANDY moans and repeats the corpse hand bit. This time he picks up a whole handful of chocolates and stuffs them into his mouth. He moans as he chews them, then he puts the bedcovers over his head. He stays there. Then the hand comes out from under the covers for another chocolate. Pause. Head comes out again.)* Oh, my Jeezez, oh. Oh. Oh. Oh. Oh, my Jeezez. *(Pause. Lifts head as if to tell his story. He changes his mind, and his head falls back on the pillow.)* Ah, shag it. I couldn't be bothered. *(He speaks laconically to the audience:)* Do you ever get so depressed you can feel it in your hands? Like the palms of your hands are depressed. Know what I mean? Like the wounds of Christ. The stigmata of depression. *(Defeated.)* Ahhh. *(He manages to lift himself up to rest on his elbows.)* I'm not going to tell you about how I'm thirty-five years old and I got no money and no youngsters and no one to love me. Because I couldn't be bothered. *(Falls back again. Pause.)* Anyone want a chocolate? Anybody? *(He waits until someone responds.)*

VOICE FROM AUDIENCE: Yes.

ANDY: Come on down and get it. I'm not going up there. *(Sigh. Pause. He reaches down under the covers and hauls up some magazines and newspapers. He throws the newspapers on the floor. Then he reaches down and pulls up a large can of tobacco from deep under the covers. Opens can of tobacco. Looks for rolling papers. Reaches down into bed, feels around, and pulls up an empty Kentucky Fried Chicken bucket in which he has stuffed an empty "big boss" Pepsi bottle, a Crispy Crunch wrapper, and a large chip bag.)* This, uh, this is the three stages of depression here. This *(indicating Crispy Crunch)* is uh, feeling low. *(Throws it away, then, holding up empty Kentucky Fried Chicken bucket in one hand and empty Pepsi bottle in the other:)* Severely depressed. *(Throws them away, then holds up the empty chip bag:)* Chips means you're on the mend. *(Throws chip bag away. Searches under the covers again, throws away some new papers, finds a large Raggedy Andy doll, lays it on the pillow next to him. He reaches down again, finds rolling papers, and rolls a cigarette as he continues to talk.)* He's on the rollies now. Of course, I suppose everybody is. I wonder what the Jesuit fathers in St. John's would think if they could see me now. Rolling cigarettes and eating chocolates down in a dirty syphilitic hall in downtown St. John's. You know what I say? *(Beat.)* I say shag 'em. I'd say shag ye too, except I've got to be nice to the audience. My mother always said, "Be nice to the audience." *(A furry, rat-like creature scurries from under the bed out into the wings.* **ANDY** *throws a book at it.)* Ah, shag it. *(The rat is a poorly made prop—obviously a piece of fluff pulled on a string by someone offstage.)* That's the prop rat there.

Anybody got a light? Anybody? Got a match? Nobody? *(He waits until an audience member throws him a matchbox; if the matchbox is out of reach, he looks at it for a few seconds, then turns to the audience.)* Anybody else got a match? *(Waits while matches land on various parts of the stage. It is obvious he isn't getting out of bed. Finally, one pack of matches or a lighter actually lands on the bed.)* Thanks. *(He lights the cigarette. Relaxes into his pillow. Beat.)*

Well…*(cigarette cough)*, this is it, this is the show. What do you think so far? Having a good time or what? *(He coughs again. Beat. He whistles "Strangers in the Night" for a few seconds, then coughs violently over the edge of the bed and spits into a piece of newspaper. Crumples up paper, doesn't know what to do with it. Puts it under the covers.)* Suppose I'll get any groupies out of the show tonight? I suppose they'll be flocking around me. *(In a St. John's–Mom voice:)* "And why wouldn't they?" That's what my mother'd say to me all the time. "Why wouldn't they? Shur, you're gorgeous. *(Beat.)* You've got lovely teeth."

Mom always accentuated the positive. I do have nice teeth, though, luh. *(Shows his teeth.)* Nice? Lovely brown eyes. *(He bats his eyes at the audience, then suddenly becomes quite chatty.)* It's funny, it's funny what you think you look like, sometimes—kind of your *mental image* of what you look like. I know I've got a certain kind of mental image of myself, and every time I walk by a mirror, I get an awful shock. I sort of think of myself of having kind of classic Hollywood good looks, you know? I mean, like—not that looks are important or anything—but I just happen to be blessed with Hollywood good looks. The kind of, uh—Jesus, not the Robert Redford look, right? I know I can't stand the look of Robert Redford. I don't know why people say he's so good-looking. Every time I see him, I always think of a cheese sandwich. You know what I mean? He's got that kind of yellow look about him, it's like a cheese sandwich on white bread. And he's got those little pimples on his face, you know, like a cheese sandwich with pimples on it. Like someone left their lunch in the operating room after minor surgery. (*Pause. He sighs a big sigh.*) That was the joke I made up for the show tonight. (*Beat.*) Things are warming up a bit, anyway.

I think of myself as looking more like, uh, what's his name, the guy that's in *Cool Hand Luke*? (*Asking the audience:*) What's his name? Paul Newman, right. Only maybe with like…a scar on my face or something. And then I walk past a mirror somewhere and I realize I've got a perfect bowling-ball head. If I had three little holes here (*indicating his eyes and mouth*), I'd be a perfect bowling ball. A bowling-alley body and little toes for pins. (*He twiddles his bare toes that are sticking out at the bottom of his blanket. Sighs. Turns on the radio for a few seconds; elevator music plays. He arranges blankets, smooths them out, looks at audience for a long time. Nothing. Turns the radio off, becomes a little enthusiastic.*) I was going to do a show like I was in Denmark, right? And I was going to have like a big map of Newfoundland, and I'd tell the audience—the Danish audience—where Newfoundland was. And I was going to have the programs printed in Danish and stuff, right? (*Pause, sigh.*) That was a good idea… And then I was thinking about doing like a real jazzy song-and-dance type show, right? Fred Astaire and Ginger Rogers–type thing…But I was so depressed I couldn't get the tuxedo together. (*Beat, then very offhand:*) We're going to have an explosion now. It's not going to be a very big one, but if you have a heart condition or anything, be forewarned. (*Then, to the stage manager up in the booth at the back of the audience:*) John-Paul, whenever you're ready. (*Huge explosion in the garbage can extreme left.*)

The director thought something should happen about now. John-Paul got that together for us. (*Nod to the stage manager.*)

I was thinking...another idea I had...was having speakers all over the theatre, right, and have a big helicopter noise, and that. Like it'd sound like a helicopter flying overhead, and the sound would go from speaker to speaker. *(The sound effect of helicopter moves from speaker to speaker.)* Like that, right. *(Helicopter fades. Beat, sigh.)* That was a good idea too. *(Silence, pause; he sighs, tries to think of something.)*

Yeah, well, I could play with the lights for a while. *(Playing with lights like an orchestra conductor, he makes them go intense, then fade; then he makes stage right light up, then stage left, etc. He makes spooky magic sounds:)* Woooo... Woooo...Woooo...Woooo...*(Then he makes a whistling sound like a spaceship landing in an old movie. Finally, he directs the lights to go to different places by making popping sounds.)*

Pretty good, hey? Big hand for John-Paul there. *(Audience applauds the stage manager's light show.)* Look, I don't want anybody coming back after the show and saying they liked the show, or they didn't like the show, or this should be cut, or this was too long. Because honest to God, I don't give a shit. That's one thing I'm after learning, I don't give a shit what the audience thinks. *(Looks around set.)* Obviously...

Are there any critics in the audience tonight? I don't want to see any of my jokes appearing in your columns. You can write your own goddamn columns. The critics. Spare me. They couldn't criticize an orgasm at a circle jerk. *(He sighs a big sigh.)* That's another joke I made up for the show tonight. *(Picks up a magazine, skims through it, and reads aloud:)* "Wanted, a computer programmer in Bermuda." *(He throws the magazine away in despair. Pause. Bored, he idly pulls his hair down over his forehead; makes a weak scary-ghost voice:)* Woooo...I'm not your daddy. Woooo...That was a game my father used to play with me when I was a kid. Pull his hair over his face and say, "I'm not your daddy." Another game he used to play was Johnny Goodhand and Johnny Bad-hand. Johnny Good-hand, finest kind of a fella. Would never squeeze your knee or tickle ya or cause trouble or anything.

> **ANDY** *falls for a few seconds into the character of* **UNCLE VAL,** *a seventy-five-year-old outharbour Newfoundland storyteller who speaks in a melodious northern Conception Bay accent.*

UNCLE VAL: Johnny Bad-hand, he was another story altogether. All he ever done was sit around the coal box all day long. He never washed his face, he never combed his hair, and he never shaved until he was twenty-one years of age. All he ever done *(being suspenseful:)* was take a potato, stick it on his big toe, stick it in the fire, roast it, and eat it...

ANDY: That's a character I've been doing for years called "Uncle Val."

I'd like to get up now and do a real jazzy song-and-dance routine. But I dunno. *(Beat.)* I couldn't be bothered. *(Defensive:)* Not that I couldn't do it, I tell ya. *(Hint of bitterness.)* I could show the Toronto dance crowd a thing or two. *(With great effort, he throws his legs over the side of the bed.)* Oh, Jeezez. Ow. Oh, glory be to God. *(He then stands up, revealing that he is wearing soccer shorts and is barefoot.)* Nice legs too, wha? *(He wobbles, then falls back and sits on edge of the bed.)* Oh Jeezez. *(Dizzy spell.)* Oh, I'm not hungover or anything, you know, it's just that the bloody head is gone completely. Like a band of steel around it all the time. *(Stands up once again with overly dramatic effort.)* Ah. Oh dear. Ah. Jeezez, he's up! He's up! He's not a fighting man, but he's up. Ah Jeezez, sometimes I wish I *was* a fighting man. But I'm not and that's all there is to it.

> *He immediately sits back on the edge of the bed. He has obviously given up. Beat. He decides to have a snack. He reaches across to an extension cord on the floor and plugs in the electric kettle that is on the chair next to the bed. He waits for a second, then takes a tea bag from a box in the bed and plunks it directly into the kettle. Impatiently, he feels the side of the kettle to see if it is boiled. He just can't wait.*

ANDY: Ah, shag it.

> *He unplugs the kettle, grabs a cup from the table, and pours the obviously cold water into the cup and drinks it.*

ANDY: Lovely.

Then he spies the stale sticky bun on the table. He wants it but can't reach it. He is desperate but too lazy to get up from the bedside. Sees the solution! Tries to hook the bun towards him with the electric kettle cord. That doesn't work. Then he sees the hammer. He delicately lays the kettle plug on top of the bun and, using the hammer artfully, taps the electrical plug into the bun and triumphantly hauls the bun towards himself; he grabs it, then crawls to the margarine under the table. He finds a knife on the floor and smears some margarine on his bun. He takes a big bite and discovers a little toy drum, which is also under the table. Still on his knees, he gives himself a drum roll. He succeeds in standing up with a flourish.

A NAIL UP MY NOSE

ANDY: *(With a surprising energy not seen so far,* **ANDY** *announces in the voice of a carnival barker:)* I will now drive a four-inch nail into my face!!! And, if weather conditions are permitting, I will also set fire to my own head. *(He then begins to speak in the voice of* **RICARDO HUERTA**, *a phony European with a slippery accent that might be Italian, might be Spanish.)*

RICARDO: *(Introducing the show with grand flourish:)* You heard what the man said, ladies and gentlemen! Tonight! Herren und Damen, ladies and gentlemen, in beautiful, bee-oo-ti-ful Copenhagen, capital of daring, dashing Denmark. It's *Out of the Bin!* And I'm your host, Ricardo Huerta. And believe me, ladies and gentlemen, when I say that *anything* can happen here tonight! The performer is backstage now doing his yogic preparations for the nail in the face! For the very first time in the history of human endeavour, here tonight, at the LSPU Hall, ladies and gentlemen...And here he is, "The Amazing Tub"!

ANDY: Thank you very much, Ricardo.

RICARDO: You are welcome, "Amazing Tub."

OUT OF THE BIN • 11

ANDY: *(Taking a two-and-a-half-inch nail from the table, he walks downstage and into the audience.)* Ladies and gentlemen, I am now taking this ordinary household four-inch nail and I will bring it into the audience. I will ask this gentleman right here to kindly inspect the nail, if you would please, sir. Is that in fact a genuine four-inch nail?

MEMBER OF AUDIENCE: *(Ad lib, for example:)* Well, I suppose two and a half.

ANDY: *(Ad lib, depending upon the audience response.)* Two and a half. Well, it's not too bad, sir. Two-and-a-half-inch nail. Okay, there you have it! A *genuine* nail. Now please keep your eye on the nail at all times. *(He's the showman now.)* Okay, I'm now taking the nail and I will dip it into some antiseptic Dettol that I have right here. *(Goes to table and takes a bottle of Dettol and a piece of cotton batting.)* Here I am. Keep your eye on the nail. It's the same nail. Watch me there, sir. I am now dipping the nail in the Dettol, and I will take this small bit of cotton wool here. And I will... Same nail, sir, is it?

MEMBER OF AUDIENCE: Yup.

ANDY: *(Wiping the Dettol from the nail:)* I will now clean the nail off, like so. Get the fuzzy bits off it there. Okay, I am now taking a hammer; keep your eye on the nail, and I will now drive it into my face. *(Using the hammer, he gently taps the nail straight into his horizontal nasal passage.)* There it goes. Going in. There you have it ladies and gentlemen, going in, going in. And there it is now, embedded in my face! *(He presents his face triumphantly.)* Thank you very much. And I will now remove the nail! *(Using the claw part of the hammer, he removes the nail.)* Very delicate process here. Removing the nail, very, very painful. And there you have it! Now, sir, I'll ask you, is this in fact the same nail? *(Hands audience member the nail.)* Mind the snots there, sir.

MEMBER OF AUDIENCE: Yes.

ANDY: Yes, it is! And there we have it. A four-inch nail in my face!!! (*He elicits applause.*)

OIL FOR AMERICA, PART ONE:
MOVING NEWFOUNDLAND TO ARIZONA

ANDY *walks to stage right into sharp-edged spotlight and becomes* **SENATOR GORDON GOODBAR**, *an archetypal American Southern populist Senator.*

SENATOR GORDON GOODBAR: People of New*found*land, I ain't going to talk in no fancy language or high-blown words here today. I'm going to talk straight from the hip to the people of New*found*land, and I'm going to start off by telling a little story. It is the story...of a little old lady who telephoned me, all the way from St. John's to Washington the other day. And she told me how Mayor John Murphy of St. John's was going to put a highway here and a highway there. And how he reckoned he could only preserve certain buildings of high historical significance. And that little old lady wondered what would happen to the neighbourhood that she'd been living in for forty years. So I got on the phone to Mayor Murphy. And he only said one word to me. Oil. O-I-L, oil, he said. "We've gotta do it, Senator Goodbar," he said, "so that America can have oil."

America, the greatest oil-consuming nation in the world! The greatest *everything*-consuming nation in the world! And you know, there was only one phrase that could escape 'twixt my lips, and that was "God bless you, Mayor Murphy." And then I went back to bed. But I was one troubled little Senator. And I tumbled into a troubled sleep. And I had a dream. And in that dream, I saw a lonely people living in a foggy city on a rocky coast. And off that rocky coast I saw some very peculiar-looking thingamabobs that was sucking a dirty black sludge out of the ocean. And that dirty black sludge was turning to gold in those lonely people's hands. Then I went in for a close-up. You know how sometimes you can do that in your dream. You can kind of go in for a close-up? Well, that's

OUT OF THE BIN • 13

what I did. And I saw that those people were still among the poorest white people in all of North America. And my heart broke, in my dream! I cried, in my dream!

But then I started getting practical.

And I woke up my wife, Lola, who is thirty years my junior and was lying in the bed next to me—where she should be, and where every good wife should be. And I said to her, "Lola," I said, "I'm going to move all of those people out of that cold and foggy city and move them down to the warm desert sands of Arizona." And she said to me, "Gordon," she said, "those people ain't going to want to move down to that dirty, filthy old desert."

And I said, "Never you mind, Lola," I said, "because I'm gonna build me St. John's. I'm gonna build an exact replica of St. John's, right down in the middle of the desert sands of Arizona. With the help and expertise of the Disney people, the Walt Disney people." But then to make absolutely sure, I got on the phone to y'all Prime Minister, Mr. Brian Mulroney. And you know what he said to me?

He said, "Senator Goodbar," he said, "take the whole goddamn province. The whole place is cold and poor and foggy and lonely."

And I said, "God bless you, Brian," I said. And you know, people say that man and his cabinet are in the pocket of the American government. For shame. Why, the opposite is true. Why, America is *inside him*. America is inside all Canadians! It's inside them big down-filled coats y'all wear. Inside your big woolly trousers. Wake up, Canada, America is inside you! But I digress from my story. So I got on the phone to the Disney people. The Walt Disney people. And they said to me not only would they be willing to build me New*found*land down in the desert sands of Arizona, but also they would do it for *free* if the people of St. John's would be willing to have Mickey Mouse be a kind of honorary Mayor. And I said no problem; I said those people are very familiar with Mickey, and in fact they'd probably be willin' to have Goofy be a kinda honorary premier. People of New*found*land, your troubles are over. In a little while, there ain't gonna be no St. John's and again in a little while, there ain't goin' be no New*found*land, thanks to America, to the good Lord, to

Mickey Murphy and Mayor Mouse…Oh…er, I mean Mayor Murphy and Mickey Mouse…(**SENATOR GOODBAR** *takes a bow; lights change.*)

ANDY: *(Now he begins speaking as himself, somewhat outside his earlier bedridden depression.)* That was Senator Gordon Goodbar there, and before that, "The Nail up the Nose," two hits from my past. This show is, ladies and gentlemen, a retrospective of my entire performing career. I am a small-town comedian and quite well-known to a small group of people in that small town.

My name is *(He takes a white cardboard sign from the centre stage chair and holds it up; it says ANDY JONES. He gets the audience to say it.)* Very good. I have been an actor type *(holds up a card saying COMEDIAN and gets the audience to say it)* for *(holds up a card saying ELEVEN, gets the audience to say it)* years. As if you gave a *(holds up a card saying F**K, dares the audience to say it; they generally don't).*

WHY IS THAT FUNNY? A LECTURE ON COMEDY
(WITH PERSONAL CONFESSIONS)

ANDY: Actually, my career in the theatre really began in grade three when I was in a play called *Hannibal Crosses the Alps.* I am proud to say that I played the part of Hannibal in that play. The director at that time used the "English book over the head" method of directing. A method which a lot of people think should be brought back to the Canadian theatre.

Yes, it's true, ladies and gentlemen, here tonight I'm going to give you my entire life story from grade three on. (And you paid good money.)

So, I thought what I should maybe do—to sort of spice things up a little bit—is to simultaneously give you a lecture on the "Elements of Humour." Using these cards right here.

> **ANDY** *sits at the small table downstage left, where some index cards are laid out in piles. He speaks in an earnest personal style, unfazed by the fact that the audience doesn't find much of it funny. The laughs come from his conviction that this material is funny.*

ANDY: Now last winter I went out on a humour field trip in St. John's. And I went around looking for funny things. And I actually, uh, I actually found quite a funny piece of ice. But it melted before I could get it here tonight. *(Beat.)* And that's an example of...snappy patter *(he flips over a card from pile #1)*, which is "Form of humour number one." So unbeknownst to you, the lecture has begun. *(Picks up second card from pile #1.)* And on my second card here, I have "Juxtaposition," a very, very basic form of humour. For example, "the cow is on top of the barn."

Now why is that funny? *(Looks at the audience as if expecting an answer. The audience does not find this funny, but boldly, he carries on.)* That's funny because normally speaking, you have a picture in your own mind of a cow *inside* the barn. But I've presented you with a new picture, and these two pictures laid side by side create a certain tension; this tension is in turn transferred to your body *(he mimes the two tensions side by side, then he transfers the tension by clutching his own chest)*, and then to relieve the tension—ha ha ha—you laugh. *(He mimes releasing the tension by throwing his arms outward as he gives his mirthless laugh.)* That's juxtaposition.

(He earnestly turns over the "Juxtaposition" card and picks up card #3 from the same pile.) And another generic humour umbrella would of course be "Wit." Would someone in the audience say something to me, anything at all? I'll give you a witty reply.

MEMBER OF AUDIENCE: *(Ad lib.)*

ANDY: *(Matter-of-factly:)* Uh...Eat my shorts.

An example of "Wit" there *(as he places the "Wit" card upside down on the "already seen" pile)*.

Now this lecture itself may get a little bit dry, so I'm going to spice it up a little bit by reading from this set of cards here. And these are "personal confession cards." *(Picks up pile of cards #2.)* And they're real personal confessions from my own private life. They're things which I have never told *anybody* else in my *entire life* before, but I'm going to tell you here tonight. It's true. No one has ever heard this stuff before. For example, I see personal confession card number one tells that I once wrote a love letter to Hana Gartner. *(Pause.)* You know Hana Gartner on *Take 30* on CBC?…I've been in love with Hana Gartner for years.

(Mildly worried:) The confessions get a bit better as we go on.

And at the same time, for any children in the audience or for parents looking for games to play with children on rainy afternoons, I'm going to also play "Guess the Canadian Town." *(Points to pile of cards #3.)* And I will be miming out various Canadian towns for you and asking you to guess what they are. For example, I see the first one here is…*(He picks a card from the "game" pile.)* Can you guess what the town is? *(He puts his bare foot up on the desk and picks at his big toenail.)* Anybody know?

MEMBER OF AUDIENCE: Pickering.

ANDY: What's that? Pickering, no, good guess though.

MEMBER OF AUDIENCE: Pictou.

ANDY: Pictou! Very good, very good indeed. Yes, it's a Canadian town. *(Aside:)* I wish I had a fridge or something I could give you.

All right, uh, artfully interspersed with the "Guess the Canadian Town" cards, I have "Edu-cards." *(Points to the fourth pile of cards.)* Which are survival tips for growing minds in the technological jungle. And they're quite simple things, like, for example, Edu-card number one. *(He picks it up and reads it:)* "Never take an electric radio into the bathtub with you."

This may seem obvious. But it's been a source of concern to me over the years how children learn that sort of survival tip. For example, when did you actually find out that you were not supposed to bring an electric device into the bath with you? Were you five years old? Were you six, four, three?—you know. And if it had happened a month later, it might have been too late.

There seems to be no official program for passing this on to children. So I hope to rectify that to some extent here tonight.

This is a more…I guess…serious part of the show. Just to give you an example of what I mean, I'll just try this adult bit of information: Say your car breaks down and you're getting towed by a friend and there's a rope going from your front bumper to his rear bumper. Your four wheels are on the ground. What is the last thing you got to remember to do before the towing vehicle takes off? Anyone know? Besides having the brake off and having the car in neutral and so on. Anyone know?

MEMBER OF AUDIENCE: Getting in the car?

ANDY: Getting in the car, very good sir, yes. (*Waits; no response.*) Well, it's amazing no one knows, but you must make sure you *turn the key in the ignition.* Otherwise, your steering will be locked. And so, if the towing vehicle turns, then you would keep going straight on. (*He mimes it.*) How many people in the audience tonight did not know that? (*Pleased with himself:*) I could have saved a life here tonight. (*Aside:*) I actually did that once—nearly killed my girlfriend and her aunt.

Another quick tip here—for children. "If you put your finger in the hole of a telephone jack, you can get a shock." (*Mimes the shock.*) I wouldn't have thought that. I just found that out the other day.

Another bit of interesting information for you: Bugden's Taxi in St. John's have a station-wagon service. So if you phone them up and you need a small number of things moved, rather than have to go rent a truck, they'll actually send a station wagon.

(*As an afterthought:*) And...if you want carpentry work done in St. John's, Newfoundland, call Tim Cohen or Paddy Mackey, 555–4581.

NO MAN IS AN ACTOR:
THE ARTS IN NEWFOUNDLAND, 1983

ANDY: And now it's time for Minitorial on the Arts! And your host this evening, Andy Jones. (*Switching to a slurred, drunken voice.*) Thank you. As you may or may not know, I recently retired from the Theatre. And my friends began pressing me to write my memoirs. Then I had a brilliant idea. Why not return to the stage one last time and perform my memoirs monologue-style. And here you are. And the doors are locked.

(Stops doing the drunken voice.) Actually, it's interesting being an actor in Newfoundland (sometimes) because most people don't even know that there are people living in Newfoundland who are actors. I mean, when people ask what you do for a living—most of the time, you just *lie* rather than get involved in the conversation. Seriously. I know: Charlie Tomlinson, who is the director of this show tonight (if you can believe this show was directed) was at a New Year's Eve party last year and someone asked him what he did for a living. And he said he was "an inside postal worker." And later on in the evening, when the conversation got around to the arts in St. John's, someone asked what went on down at the LSPU Hall, and he said, "I don't know."

And then the cock crew.

The scene that I always picture takes place in an outport in Newfoundland and goes something like this.

SKIPPER: *(With general rural suspicion and a hint of serial killer:)* 'Ello Mr. Jones. I see you'll be spending a few more days with us 'ere in *Snake Cove*.

ANDY: *(Naive, out of his depth:)* Yes, Skipper, God willing. Ha, ha, ha.

SKIPPER: *(With more specific suspicion:)* And what do you do for a living, Mr. Jones?

ANDY: *(Slightly plummy voice:)* I am an *Ac-tor*, Skipper.

SKIPPER: *(He knows* **ANDY** *is lying.)* Ohhh yes.

ANDY: And you know that *he* knows that you're lying. Like: "What do you mean you're an actor? If I go to the Avalon Mall cinema, do I see you on the screen? If I turn on my TV, do I see you on *Dallas*?" *(He changes fully to a* **SKIPPER** *accent.)*

SKIPPER: I did not ask you what you did in your spare time, Mr. Jones. If you asked me what I did for a living, I'd 'ardly say "I play darts," now, would I? Are you putting me off, Mr. Jones? (**SKIPPER** *is getting angry now.*) Or worse still, are you putting me *on*—with your Memorial University Extension accent. I'll show you who's an actor. Take this, Mr. Actor. (*He's getting into it now, he stands up from the table, mimes grabbing someone by the lapels and kneeing them in the groin:*) I'll show you, my little yellow-bellied friend, who's an actor. (*Mimes punching him in the guts.*) Act your way out of this. (*Repeated grunts and punches in the guts and an uppercut to the "ac-tor."*)

ANDY: (*Suddenly dropping the punch-up and sitting down:*) That's a fear that I have. But I may be a little bit paranoid, I guess.

But it is amazing that there is this breed of people who have somehow managed to survive over the past twelve or fifteen years in Newfoundland as ACTORS! It's a story that should be told. (*Speaking in pompous news-narrator voice:*) For they are, ladies and gentlemen, yes, they are "our Actors"! (*He stands proud and plummy.*) Yes, Skipper, I am an "Ac-tor."

SKIPPER: (*Now converted, he is fawning on* **ANDY**.) Oh Mr. Jones, I seen a Minitorial on actors the other day and I know what a noble breed of people they are!

ANDY: (*Singing in a plummy voice approximately to the tune of "America the Beautiful" as he mimes holding a mic on a wire:*)
Oh ac-ac-tors,
Oh ac-ac-tors,
Oh ac-tors of Newfoundland.
Oh ac-ac-tors,
Oh ac-ac-tors,
Oh yes we understand.
(*Open-mouthed, looking heavenward by the end of the song, he mimes the mic slipping out of his hand and down his throat; he holds onto the cord; he makes a weak attempt to pull it back up again, but then, accidentally, he completely swallows it and the mic goes into his guts: he gyrates his lower body to indicate the passage of the mic down through his stomach and through his bowels; he pauses; it*

seems to be over...no! Here it comes out his rear end! He mimes tugging it all the way back out of his rear end and up to his mouth to repeat the singing of the last line:) Oh yes, we understand! (He sits back at his desk; he's instantly back to business.)

That's an example of physical mime humour there. (He reaches over and matter-of-factly turns a card over from pile #1.)

And now back to "Minitorial on the Arts." And now we present a special feature on homosexuality in the arts, with special emphasis on high-placed queers in the arts industry. But first, "Ideas."

LISTER SINCLAIR: (In an earnest, academic, mid-Atlantic CBC voice, **ANDY** introduces a segment of **LISTER SINCLAIR**'s radio show called Ideas.)

Tonight!

Shoes!

Orthopedic aids or prisons of the feet? Good evening.

If you go to the laundromat to wash all your laundry, what do you wear to the laundromat?

Answer?

Shoes.

ANDY: Now time for personal confession card number two. This is actually quite a difficult confession to make. Last year, I was in Montreal for six months. And during that whole time, I had absolutely no sexual contact of any sort. And one night I went to a party, and I got very, very drunk and fell asleep on the floor. And I woke up at about five o'clock in the morning and there was a woman who had also gotten very drunk and fallen asleep and she was also on the floor very near me. And, um, and I um, I touched her breast. Just for a second! I pulled my hand back right away! I realized I'd gone too far. (Pause.) But I did actually do that.

(Not missing a beat:) And now back to Minitorial on the Arts! I'm sorry, our special on homosexuality in the arts was pre-empted by the previous scene. Ahhhhh, too bad. Ah, I'm going to check, just a second, Gerry? (To backstage:) Can we run that special on homosexuality in the arts? Ah. Ah. Awww. It's been wiped. Too bad. You should have seen it. Woo, ho, ho, ho. You would have loved it, folks. You would have died stiff as a dead snake, sir. And the pictures? Oh, woo, woo. The pics. Woo, ho, ho, ho, ho. Ho, ho. *(Shakes his hand as if it were hot, notices his own wrist is limp from hot hand gesture. Nervously throws it off.)* Aha. Actors on the march! *(Then, for no apparent reason, he suddenly returns to his slurred-voiced drunk from before.)*

DRUNKEN HOST: *(Slurring his words:)* And I'm your host. How long have you been in this business, Annie? *(Talking to himself:)* Annie? No, I said AN-DY. Oh, I though you said "Annie." Oh, God. *(Head down on table, crying).* Oh, God, I feel sick. *(Does his impressive vomiting shtick which involves the little "hech" sound—that little catch at the back of the throat, that gag-reflex click. Then, staying with the slurred voice:)* No, I'm not sick, I'm jusz an actor pretending to be sick.

ANDY: *(Snaps out of it—actor magic! Becomes himself:)* Hey! What did I tell you about versatility in the Newfoundland acting community? *(Switches again to the drunk. More actor magic.)* Oh no, God, I really am sick. *(Looks sick again. Burps, smells burp; this makes him feel better; he switches to an obnoxious, cool-guy voice:)* Hey, I was just an actor pretending to be drunk, and pretending to be pretending to be sick. *(Phony actor smile.)* Ha, ha, ha, ha, ha. What about this guy, huh? *(Returns to his own voice:)* The vomiting that you just saw in that scene comes under the heading of "Special Talents." *(Turns over a card from the third pile.)* And these are the kinds of "Special Talents" I had all my life.

THE SHITTING PIG: A SPECIAL TALENT

You laugh, but it's kind of sad that the kinds of insights that I had—even as a young boy—were along those lines. I realized very early in life that when people vomited, they didn't just go "blaaaaa." *(He does the bland, ordinary, single-protrusion-of-the-tongue vomit gesture.)* I noticed the little "hech" *(he again does that little catch at the back of the throat, that gag-reflex click)* BEFORE the "yeeeeech." I was burdened with the knowledge of the click *(he repeats the gag-reflex "hech"),* that little extra catch. Hech…Hech.

That's the kind of insight I had. It was sad to watch all my friends go off and become lawyers and doctors and so on, and even though I realized that I could have done those things, I could *never* have done those things as well as I could do things like vomiting. *(In response to laughter:)* No! It was really quite sad. I'm tryin' to make a serious point here—what I am saying is: I could have done those other things; I could have been a member of the House of Assembly; I could have been a doctor—but *anybody* could do those things. But very, very few people could do...*(he does his amazingly skillful vomiting shtick again).*

(He rises from his seat, in a ridiculously emotional, mock-triumphant pose, providing his own fanfare.) I realized that this is my talent. Yes, ladies and gentlemen, this is my talent. *(Singing a triumphant fanfare:)* Bump pa bum! Bumpa pa bump pa bum! This is the beauty that I will leave behind me after I die. Bum, pa-bum. *(He is marching now to his own drummer.)* Late night poo-poo ca-ca jokes. Bump pa bum! Bumpa pa bump pa bum! This is my talent! Bum, pa-bum. *(A cry from the heart:)* I was almost boy of the year at Gonzaga, *(aside:)* Gonzaga High School, for the Danish audience. Bum, pa-bum. I'm sorry, Father MacKenna; I'm sorry, Brother Molloy. But this is my talent! Bum, pa-bum, pa, pa, pa-bum, pa-bum. Things like...the Shitting Pig! *(He stops marching; he makes a pig nose, then a slushy shitting sound and then reaching between his legs, he mimes catching and eating his own shit.)* Bum, pa-bum. *(Then, calling out in an admiring fan's voice from his past:)* Do the Shitting Pig again, Andy! *(He does. Again, the admiring voice:)* Beautiful, man, beautiful! *(Marching in place:)* Bum, pa-bum, pa, pa, ba-bum, ba-bum. I vomit! *(He stops and vomits.)* Bum, pa-bum. I vomit on the audience! *(Goes into front row and mimes vomiting on audience.)* Bum, pa-bum. I sneeze *(he stops and sneezes)*; I cough *(coughs)*; I fart *(farts)*; I burp *(burps)*. I do them all together *(simultaneous sneeze, cough, fart, burp)*. Bum pa-bum. I tempt fate. Bum pa-bum. I lick my tongue out at cancer. *(With protruding tongue and to the same tune as the "bum pa bums")* Nya, nya-nya, nya, nya, nya, nya-nya, nya-nya. I challenge God to strike me dead by saying things like "Jesus was a fag!" Ah, ahhhhhhh. *(Screams. He is struck to the ground by God; he gets his glasses and makes his eyes bulge ridiculously by putting the plastic-lens sections in the flesh under his eyes; then he twists his body*

and says in his "stroke-victim" voice:) I said that Jesus was a fag down at the LSPU Hall and then I had a stroke. *(Stroke-victim laugh:)* Heh heh, heh. *(Pleading piteously:)* But I'm still a funny guy. Please, please let me back on the stage again, please, please! *(Returns to himself; starts to break into a real crying jag, but sings through the tears:)* Bum-ba, bum, ba, ba, ba, ba-bum, ba-bum.

(He's sobbing quietly now:) Yes, this is my talent. But nobody wants to come down and see it. Not down at the LSPU Hall. The only place in the world you can get syphilis without having sexual intercourse. I'm sick of it. I'm sick of begging people to come down and see me. The brown-tongued theatre of North America. *(Wailing, then crying foolishly, bitterly:)* I don't care! Don't come down and see me! Don't see me pour my guts out! Don't see the brightest and the best. *(In the middle of his crying, he suddenly switches into sycophantic begging.)* Please. Please come down and just see one show. Please? I know it's kind of dirty down there, but I think you'll like it. I'll give you a free ticket! *(Quiet, resigned sobbing as he hears that admiring fan's voice in his head again:)*

"Do the Shitting Pig again, Andy, you'll feel better."

"Okay." *(He does a sad, slowed-down version of the Shitting Pig through his tears.)* "Beautiful!"

(Sad, melodramatic, tragic:) It *is* beautiful too. I have dedicated my life to beauty.

(Switches quickly back to his own voice, as if this has all been part of the "Lecture on Comedy.") That's uh…nauseating self-pity humour, there. *(Matter-of-factly, he turns over a card and carries on with his lecture.)*

THE SOFT-SPOT MURDERER

Okay. Now, back to "Guess the Canadian Town." *(Looks closely at the card.)* Ah, Dildo, forget it. Edu-card number two. *(Reading card:)* "Infantile death often results from touching the sublingual artery with exposed electrical devices." In other words, don't put your child's tongue in a light socket. This can be a source of humour in itself. And it would be called "black humour." For example, the Soft-Spot Murderer. You know the soft spot that children have on their heads when they're born. (*Touches the top of his head*) Picture a nursery in a St. John's hospital, little children asleep in rows of cots, and up comes...the Soft-Spot Murderer! (*With his murderous index finger ready, he does exaggerated "sneaking-up" movements as he makes radio mystery music climax sounds:*) Dant dant dant dant daaaa da da da da! (*A quick breath, then he mimes his index finger poking down, deep into a soft spot:*) Sploosh! (*He repeats the whole sequence.*) Dant dant dant dant daaaa da da da da sploosh!

Not so funny for parents with small children. (*Puts the card back on the pile.*) But a genuine example of black humour.

Okay, special talent B. (*Turns over a card from pile #3.*) Things like my "pulley-clothesline noise." (*He mimes advancing a clothesline on a pulley wheel as he makes that screechy sound that pulley clotheslines always make:*) Gargenzee Geegenzee Googenzee; Gargenzee Geegenzee Googenzee. (*No reaction from audience.*) Okay, just close your eyes, you're out in the backyard and this is what you hear: "Gargenzee Geegenzee Googenzee." Okay, you guys try it. Just say "Gargenzee Geegenzee Googenzee" in a high-pitched voice. Everybody all together, one, two, three: "Gargenzee Geegenzee Googenzee." That's pretty good. Maybe it's easier than I thought. Okay, the pulley-clothesline noise. (*Turns over that card and picks up the next special talent card.*) Okay, animal imitations. Very popular with children. Anyone want to see my Giant Budgie? Nobody?

AUDIENCE: Yeah, yeah.

ANDY: Okay, Giant Budgie. (*With eyes ablaze and thumbs hooked under his armpits, he flaps his elbows and bottom-lip whistles loudly and very aggressively; then the whistling, elbow-flapping Giant Budgie leaps onto the table, resting on his haunches. He slows his wing-flapping—staring and whistling menacingly at the audience in a lower register. Then he climbs down from the table and returns to the cards.*)

Giant Budgie. (*Turns over the card.*) How about my codfish? (*He does his codfish lazzi by sticking out his jaw and his bottom lip; then, while the jaw is protruding, the bottom lip comes back to touch the top lip, making a puckering sound.*

All the while, his eyes dart back and forth in googly cod style as his extended hand undulates in front of him like the tail of a fish.)

Budgie again? No? And the next card, okay.

INFURIATING HUMOUR

*Picking up a humour card, **ANDY** stares hard at it, trying to make out what is written there. He reads aloud, slowly, phonetically, as if wondering how these combinations of letters can ever result in our pronunciation of these words.*

ANDY: Tee...was. T was. Te-was. 'Twas *(got it! :)* 'Twas! *(Next word:)* Tee-hee. Tuh-hu, tee-h, th, *(got it! :)* the! 'Twas the...*(Next word:)* Nyj head. Nick-hitched, nitched, nyj-head, nicht, nix, ni-jh, *(got it! :)* night! 'Twas the night...*(Next word:)* Bay for ah. Bay for ah. Befor-ah. Befor ah, *(got it!:)* before! 'Twas the night before *(Next word:)* Sure ist is mast. Shurtismas. Christi a imus. Shirst a miss, shirst, chrsta mus, *(got it! :)* Christmas! *(Next word:)* Double-U hen. Wah hen. Wah hen, wh hen *(got it! :)* when! 'Twas the night before Christmas when...*(Next word:)* Ah lala. A ll la...all, *(got it! :)* all! When all...*(Oh no, he's in despair at the next word:)* Throw you-ga-ja. Throw you je. Throw, throu ga, *(got it:)* through! When all through... *(Next word:)* T'he, T-he again, thh, the, *(got it:)* the. When all through the... *(Next word:)* Ho youz. *(Thinks he's got it, even though it doesn't make sense:)* Ho youz! When all through the ho youz...no, that can't be right, when all through the *(getting it finally:)* house! *(Puts card down quickly.)*

An example of "Infuriating Humour."

Okay? I'm now onto the sight gag! *(Holds up a tiny knitted baby's mitten.)* Tiny mitten. Funny? *(Waits; no reaction from audience.)* Okay, how about tiny shorts? *(Holds up a tiny pair of doll's shorts, waits for reaction:)* Sight gag. Hmmm. *(He is disappointed in the audience.)*

Okay, and now onto "simple physical humour." And the simplest physical humour I guess would be what I call the finger diddle. *(Hand upright, with index finger sticking up, he wiggles it up and down.)* Do you find that funny? Anyone out there find that funny? *(Usually someone inadvertently laughs; he seizes on the laugh and moves towards that person.)* Do you find that funny, ma'am? Look, look, she's delirious, look! *(He moves towards her.)* She's backing up. Okay, ma'am is *this* funnier? *(He wiggles two fingers, she laughs more.)* Then *this* must be hilarious! *(He wiggles all ten fingers up and down:)*...Hmmm, not necessarily. *(He's learned something.)* Okay.

    (Switches to the confession card piles.) And now back to "Personal Confessions." I was a bisexual until all my gay friends told me there was no such thing. *(Quickly switches to "Guess the Canadian Town" cards.)* And now back to "Guess the Canadian Town." Here it is, next Canadian town... *(He pulls his own tongue forward with thumb and index finger, then mimes pulling it out much farther, as if it is elastic:)* Eeeeeeeow *(then mimes letting it pang back into his mouth again; with each pang he says:)* "Boy-oy-oy-oy-oing." *(He repeats this mime a number of times.)* *(Out:)* Eeeeeeeow. *(In:)* Boy-oy-oy-oy-oing. *(Out:)* Eeeeeeeow. *(In:)* Boy-oy-oy-oy-oing. Anyone know? *(Repeats.)* *(Out:)* Eeeeeeeow. *(In:)* Boy-oy-oy-oy-oing? *(Nobody gets it.)* Pangnirtung! Not that well-known a Canadian town. How about this one? *(With his thumbs growing out of his temples, his fingers make a pair of antlers. Then he juts out his jaw as far as it will go.)*

MEMBER OF AUDIENCE: Moose Jaw.

ANDY: Moose Jaw, very good. How about this one? *(Mimes a prize fighter boxing, then washing his own face.)* Come on.

MEMBER OF AUDIENCE: Do it again.

ANDY: *(He does it again.)* Pugwash. Okay, and now back to personal confession number three. This time it's your turn. Anyone in the audience who has been unfaithful to their spouse in the last week, put up their hands, please. Put up your hands, come on. *(Threatening:)* I'll have to use the "Magic Flashlight." *(Picks up a flashlight and shines it at the audience, going back and forth across the rows.)* Okay. *(In a seance voice:)* Pooley, Pooley, tell me truly, who's been slapping the make so drooly. A lot of red faces out there! Okay, who was unfaithful to their spouse in the last week and lied

about it! (*Aiming the flashlight across the audience once again:*) Ohhh. Okay...
who's been DOING IT FOR YEARS?! Even more red faces out there. A lot
of red-faced lawyers out there tonight.

Okay now, finally: anyone in the audience want to tell a joke? Does
anyone know any jokes to tell, of any sort? Here's your big chance; the
critics are here tonight.

MEMBER OF AUDIENCE: I have a Franz Kafka joke.

ANDY: Okay.

MEMBER OF AUDIENCE: Knock, knock.

ANDY: Who's there?

MEMBER OF AUDIENCE: (*says nothing*)

ANDY: That's a good joke. (*Turns over another card.*) An example of "ama-
teur humour" there.

(*He stands up.*) Don't forget: for your carpentry needs: Paddy Mackey
and Tim Cohen, 555–4581!

(*Then there is a change of tone as he returns to his self-aggrandizing "career
retrospective" tone.*) Okay, my first professional job in the theatre came in
Newfoundland with the Newfoundland Travelling Theatre Company in
1972, when I played a Munchkin in *The Wizard of Oz*. And I also played
a bishop in the adult play during that tour. And one night I went on
stage as the bishop, and a child in the audience said, "Look, there's one
of the Munchkins." After I left the Newfoundland Travelling Theatre
Company, I went to Toronto with Bob Joy, who later became the quite
well-known film actor, Robert Joy. And I got a job, and he didn't. (*Evil
laugh.*) But then he got a job, and I didn't. (*Crestfallen. His sobs return.*) And
he got another job, and another job, and another job. Then I went back
to Newfoundland, and I worked on stage with CODCO, with Mary
Walsh, Tommy Sexton, Greg Malone, and they got their own TV series.

And you know why? *(Full-throttle sobbing self-pity:)* 'Cause they sucked me dry! *(Holds up one of the big white signs that says: "And called me Dusty.")*

RICARDO'S ORIGIN STORY, PART ONE: PIT OF VIPERS

RICARDO: *(With Hollywood sincerity, a big toothy smile, and his phony Italian accent, he glosses over* **ANDY***'s self-pity:)* Let's hear it, for the comedian, ladies and gentlemen. *(Elicits applause.)*

Beautiful to see, and lovely to look at, ladies and gentlemen, fantastic, the comedian here playing the retro perspective of his *entire* life, here tonight. *(He rolls his eyes. Looks at door where* **ANDY** *has presumably gone off.)* Beautiful, beautiful. I'm Ricardo Huerta; I am your host for this evening. *(Taking them into his confidence:)* And I'm quite well-known, actually, in theatrical circles in Newfoundland, at least I was quite a few years ago...*(***RICARDO** *quickly changes the subject:)* But we are *not* here tonight, ladies and gentlemen, to talk about me! We are here tonight to do *Out of the Bin*. The performer is backstage now. Uh. *(Realizes that* **ANDY** *has disappeared. Looks at the audience. Pause. Checks once again to see that* **ANDY** *has truly disappeared. Walks close to the audience. Hangs his head in shame.)*

Ladies and gentlemen, I want to apologize for the show tonight. You know, the Newfoundland government asked me to come and to set this tour up across Denmark. But I had *no idea* this was the kind of show it was going to be. *(Pause. A disapproving snort. Sotto voce.)* "The Shitting Pig" *(making fun of* **ANDY***'s "Shitting Pig" stance)* and the "nail in the face," and such. I don't find it very funny, you know? And there he's got this dirty, filthy bedroom here. And he's got, you know, he's got the rag doll in the bed, you know? He making you think, okay, what's he doing with the rag doll in the bed, right? You know, he's making the dirty parts of the brain to turn over. I don't like theatre which activates the dirty parts that way, you know? I like, when I go to the theatre, I want to see...*(His vision:)* I want to see the kings and princes like in Shakespeare, with the long flowing gowns, and the little crowns on top of their heads, somehow. That sort of thing, you know? But, but this sort of thing here, you know? I don't want to see this, you know?

And when I first went to Newfoundland, I said to myself: "Find out what these people are about! Go to the theatre, the mirror of reality."

But Newfoundland is not like this, you know. Cursing and swearing and peeing on stage and things. You can see that at home for free, you know? But I'll tell you *(he draws them in very close for confidential material)*, he can get away with this in Newfoundland. Oh yeah, oh, they love to see that there, you know. Do you know why? Because he is a Newfoundlander! You see, I could never get away with that.

(Even more confidential:) Don't listen to him about Newfoundland; I'll tell you a thing or two about that place, you know.

Because, y'know, I'll tell you the Real Truth. I am a Newfoundlander myself. *(Insisting:)* It's true, yeah. I am a Newfoundlander. I was born as Ricardo Reardon in St. John's. And I was…no, this is true…when I was five years old, I was selling hockey tickets in front of Woolworth's on Water Street. And I was stolen by the gypsies! That's true. One minute I was selling hockey tickets in front of Woolworth's and days later I was in a crowded piazza in Italy. And the old women would come up to me and say *(in fake nonsense Italian)*, comise bruto, muchacho corionelo, paucissimi bambini. And all I could say was *(in an innocent little child's Italian accented voice:)* "do you want to buy a hockey ticket?"

(He then bravely pulls himself out of his self-pity jag.) Of course, I'm not here tonight to talk about me, ladies and gentlemen: no, the performer is coming back on again. *(With obvious disrespect to **ANDY** offstage:)* Hey just one minute, hey, I want to talk to the audience. Just a minute! *(High pitched:)* Okay justaminute! All right. *(His anger turns to a big phony smile, then suddenly a look of personal gastrointestinal disgust comes from within his body. It is heartburn.)* Oh shit, I've got really bad heartburn tonight. *(He burps spectacularly.)*

Oh. Before we flew to Copenhagen yesterday, we were in St. John's, the capital of Newfoundland. Beautiful capital city. We were eating dinner there in the historic downtown with all these fancy restaurants there—with all the sanded floors, all the bricks exposed, all the coloured lamps that hang down with little coloured pieces of glass and so on… beautiful places…*(confidentially)* but the food is shit in these places. Last

night we were eating dinner and I ordered a plate of slimes...not *slimes!*...
no, *snails, snails,* sorry...and I was eating the snails and I had eaten about
fifteen or twenty of them, but they were covered in a sauce and I didn't
know they were green—they had gone bad! And I was eating these
green slimes for half an hour, and every time I was burping *(he burps
amazingly, grossly),* a green fog was coming out of my mouth. *(He mimes
the fog.)* Green fog.

But *(he returns to phony pleasant laughter),* but I'm sorry, you don't want
to hear about this, ladies and gentlemen. Of course, I want to say, "Welcome to the show!" *(He moves closer to the audience.)* As a matter of fact, it's
actually written into my contract that I'm not to talk about my own personal problems on the stage tonight. *(Indignant:)* Can you imagine that?

It's written into my contract! I'm not, for example, to mention my wife,
Carla. You've probably read about Carla in the papers. Big scandal. She
is now living, of course, as you probably know, with Ricardo Montalban.
(Under his breath:) With the big fuckin' white hat; I could kill him.

Yes! I can't mention that. Can you imagine, a theatrical contract that
tells a man *(revving up again)* he must take a buzz saw, open up his chest,
and tear out by the roots and tendrils the memory of the only woman he
ever loved? Except of course for that landlady in Barcelona.

But you know I was thinking, you know, before the show, about the
days when Carla first left me, and I would go home by myself at the end
of the day, and I would see my little performing children in bed asleep.
The Rickettes, they're called. And I used to see them lying there—two little Rickettes in one bed, and another Rickette in another bed, and little
Tamale, the blind Rickette, in another bed.

And their little cheeks glowing like hot hamburgers in the snow!
(He's over the edge now.) And of course, I would have to go in and rattle
them awake! To tell them how miserable their life was!

Then I would have to go back to my own little room very much like
this one here. And I would sit on the edge of the bed *(he does so)* and I
would swear that I could hear Carla laughing in the great houses of
Europe. Ha, ha, ha! Like that song on the radio. *(Now in a swamp of self-
pity:)* And I could see her, I could actually see her in the long, flowing

dresses that she always wore, with her hair piled high on top of her head, filled with apple blossoms and twigs, like a giant Russian fruit salad! And the shoes she always wore *(enjoying his shoe fetish)* with the little hole in the front for the toes to peek out. And the little criss-cross straps that she always wore that pinched the alabaster plumpness of her calves.

Nooo, I'm not to mention any of that, ladies and gentlemen! *(He is flying high now, very dramatic, angry at life.)* Because of course the performer is never meant to tell the audience that he has just crawled from the slime of his personal life—still reeking of the stench of the quicksand of his shattered dreams. No, no, no. It's on with the show. The tinsel, the glitter, the lights! And the life! *(Suddenly sadly philosophical:)* And in that life, a little glimpse of the ongoing march towards death that each performer portrays for the audience in return for the laughter and applause, those tainted pieces of silver that drive him farther on, and yet at the same time knock him back into the pit of vipers. *(Throws himself backwards, spits out the next words into the audience's face:)* That pit of vipers rimmed with the jeering, mocking faces of the cruel, heartless voyeurs that are his audience.

(Realizing that he has just insulted the audience, he breaks into another toothy smile.) Now I can truly say, ladies and gentlemen, "Welcome to the show," on behalf of the government of Newfoundland. But the performer *(then to* **ANDY** *who is meant to be offstage and wanting to come back:)* yes, just a second please—here he is, he's coming back now, ladies and gentlemen, so please let me set the scene for you.

The place: Newfoundland, *(waxing poetic)* that beautiful green emerald amid the turquoise sea—with an extra bit of emerald attached to the mainland. Yes, Newfoundland, land of aching beauty where the fragile blue of the snow struggles with the emerging pentimento of spring's verdancy. It is an urgent struggle, for summer only lasts as long as the last gasp of the black northern codfish as it dies its death agony in the hold of the fish murderer's trap skiff. *(He is proud of that image.)* The place: a small outport. The room: the bedroom of the parish priest, Reverend Dennis Dinn. He writes the last sermon he will ever write as a legitimate parish priest—and the greatest sermon of his life.

FATHER DINN: (*An archetypal, scary St. John's Catholic orator/priest*) And he was taken from that place and cast into the "other place," and there every part of his body which had offended the Lord burst into flames and burned for eternity. (*Beat.*) Good afternoon, boys and girls.

RICARDO: (*Sits at the kitchen table, picks up a pen, and holds it over a sheet of paper.*) No, the priest is stuck; he looks desperately for inspiration. He thinks first of his own sermons of the past and thinks particularly of the sermon he gave the year before, on the feast of St. Patrick:

THE IRISH FACTOR: FATHER DINN ON ST. PATRICK

FATHER DINN: (*His sermons are always a roller coaster of theatrical mood swings that keep his parishioners on their toes. He is especially accomplished in the terrifying "Has the Priest Gone Mad?" preaching technique.*) If you are Irish, come into the parlour. There is a welcome there for you. (*He blesses himself.*) In the name of Father and of the Son and of the Holy Ghost. (*Calmly:*) If you are Irish, come into the parlour; there is a welcome there for you. (*Less calmly:*) If you are Irish, come into the parlour; there is a welcome there for you. (*Suddenly switching to a calculated and well-practised emotional terror tactic as he yells:*) Iffffff!!!!!!!!!...If!!!...you are IRISH!!! (*With utter disdain for the non-Irish of the world:*) Not English. Not Scottish. Not German. Not some godless primitive in a village at the mouth of the Amazon River, not some foreign sailor wasting his God-given seed on the bed of a St. John's prostitute in a mindless retrograde tryst of I'll-give-you-money-you-give-me-the-use-of-your-sexual-organs-chickey-chickey-bang-bang...(*Beat.*) Not that!...(*calmer now:*) Not a Cornish bus driver...

But if you are *Irish*...

COME!!!...Don't GO! Into the parlour. (*Slowly winding up again:*) Not the kitchen. Not the woodshed—not a mixed sauna in atheistic Russia! Not a dirty birth-control clinic in a metropolitan St. John's Protestant Hospital! (*Calm again.*) But the parlour. And we all know what the "parlour" means here in Newfoundland, don't we? There's a welcome there for you. *(On the edge again:)* Not for Hitler! Or for Chernenko! Or for Queen Elizabeth!!! *(Calm again:)* But for you. If, IF!!!...you are Irish.

RICARDO: No, this is not the inspiration the priest is looking for. He goes to his shelf and looks through his books of great sermons of the world. He sees the sermons of Bishop Roche, Bishop Howley, Hughey Shea, Rasputin—ah, his eye is caught by a slim volume. He takes it out. Is it a slim volume? No, it is a cassette tape. He puts it into his tape recorder and listens to the tape. *(**ANDY** puts it into the tape recorder and listens to the tape; after the taped introduction he takes over and does the sermon "live.")*

TAPE VOICE: And now with Yuletide messages, here's the Reverend P. Percival Freep.

TALES OF MEANNESS: REVEREND FREEP'S CHRISTMAS MESSAGE

REVEREND FREEP: (**FREEP** *is a pinched, bitter man of God of the Protestant persuasion.*) Not since my first Christmas as a student at the Guber and Winifred Stanfield School of Bible Technology in Colorado Springs, when I discovered one of my professors inebriated, dressed in women's undergarments and sprawled lasciviously at the foot of the common room Christmas tree, has the true meaning of Christmas become as clear to me as it did on Water Street the other night, when I was approached by a great, fat molasses bun of a man covered with a glaze of sweat that defied the bitterness of the winter air with a fortitude only equalled by that of his little piggy raisin eyes, in their ongoing battle not to be swallowed up by the folds of fat which surrounded them.

"Give me money," he slurred, "it's Christmas."

"On the contrary," I shot back. "You give *me* money because it's Christmas. You give *me* money back for all the alcohol and drug abuse programs I've contributed to over the last year. Time to turn the tide." I smirked. "'Tis Christ-tide," I went on, warming ardently to my mission. "'Tis Christ-tide, 'tis Christ-tide, time to pay back for favours received!"

By now I had a firm grip on his lapels and was centimetres away from his puffy, pie-like face.

"Give me, give me," I screamed, filled with the knowledge of both my physical superiority over the man and the logical bind my quick wit had twisted him into—both powers, of course, gifts from the Lord.

"I haven't got anything," he whimpered. "Thass why I asked you."

"Haven't got anything? Haven't got anything!" I laughed. "Look at the birds in the air. Look at the lilies of the field. Do they say 'I haven't got anything'?" And when the man looked up to see if he could see the birds of the air, I whipped off his coat and was away with it in a flash.

Later, in the warmth of the rectory, I pondered. What caused the throbbing warmth of satisfaction that now pulsated through my body? Was it simply the thrill of a trick well executed? The joy of just revenge on a human parasite? Nay. It was neither of these. It was because Christmas had given me the "Strength of the Justified," just as it had so many Christmases before, when my Bible school professor tried to weaken me by muttering shamefully, "We all have our weaknesses, Percy," as he stood in front of me in his tainted and garish female attire. But I was strong then too, as I boldly rang the general assembly bell that brought the entire student body to witness his eternal shame.

My actions that night paved the way for the more rigid screening processes that are in effect at Bible Technology Schools across North America, as well as hurling a bad man out into the night, teaching a whole school that you can *never* let down your guard, and seeing the true meaning of Christmas manifesting itself in my inspired rigidity...

As I thought back to those days, I walked over to the coat that I had torn off the back of the man on Water Street (with the strength of ten men). And do you know what I found? Money. Money in the pocket!! The man had *lied* to me, in addition to his other denials of the human spirit. He had kept money from a man of the cloth even though the season was Christ-tide...Sixty-two cents.

As I walked towards the youth centre canteen, I felt that no money I had ever received from any collection plate was more mine to do with as I pleased than that sixty-two cents. I took out my canteen key, opened the door, dropped the money in the till, and reached into the freezer for two pineapple Popsicles, my little reward for acting on the true meaning of Christmas. Later, as I passed by the boys' choir room, I heard them singing what I felt in my heart at that moment, as I bit into my Popsicle. The words of their song? The feeling that I had? Why, one and the same. Goodwill towards men. Thank you. Merry Christmas.

RICARDO: That was it, the inspiration the priest was looking for! He sits down, and in a matter of hours he has finished his sermon. But first, he sends it to a friend of his, a very, very old friend who suffers from the worst fate of the outport Newfoundlander: exile in St. John's. His friend replies.

BAYMAN IN EXILE: UNCLE VAL ON ST. JOHN'S

UNCLE VAL: *(In his aged voice and his gentle northern Conception Bay accent, he speaks aloud the words of the letter as he writes.)*
Dear Father Dinn,

Thank you for your sermon on Sin. As you know, I am still here in St. John's. Sometimes I feel like writing to you and saying, "Help, I am a prisoner in St. John's!" But I know you'd think: There goes that melodramatic old fool again. But I'm quite serious. People in St. John's are very strange. They keep saying things like: "There's nothing like a cup of tea in the woods."

(Deeply puzzled:) I mean, they say that quite often.

I keep picturing a cup of tea all by itself in the woods, and I agree there would be nothing quite like that.

I am living here with my daughter, Margaret. She married a man from St. John's. I tried to stop her from marrying Bernard, but I could not at that time present a coherent case. It was more instinctual. I instinctually hated Bernard. Bernard is in Insurance. Insurance is in Bernard. In fact, I believe Insurance is up Bernard—he walks kind of funny.

And their youngsters, oh my, oh my... Jimmy and Kimmy. Rhyming youngsters. Children are funny in St. John's. Here they learn by *asking questions*. Now, in my day, you did not ask questions. I mean, you had questions inside you, but you had to sit around the kitchen 'til someone accidentally expelled an answer which you then joined to a question, jigsaw-style. Sometimes, there'd be three or four youngsters sitting on the daybed, and someone would let fly with a piece of information... you could almost hear the wheels turning. (**VAL**'s *eyes glow.*) And their little eyes would glow with enlightenment. (*In the voice of the enlightened child:*) "So that's how Elizabeth come to be living at the Pottles'."

Often that was how Elizabeth herself found out.

And in those days, children *ran messages.* That was their job. And in return they were allowed to sleep indoors.

But children nowadays! It's all Spider-Man, *Dukes of Hazzard,* and Chef Boyardee Scarios. I'd give 'em a scario. (*Getting carried away:*) I'd like to go into their bedroom in the middle of the night and say, "Jimmy, Kimmy, wake up. Spider-Man is dead! Yes, they finally got 'en. He's lying out in some cheap, second-rate funeral home now, just like you will be someday. Your little white bodies laid out in little white coffins—and the skin that was once your flesh will slither off your skull and be eaten by worms." (*He smiles a big smile.*) Then they'd take notice of their grandfather. But I never say nothing. Not in St. John's.

Trusting that your bunions are better,

I remain,

Your friend,

Val.

P.S. I have no doubt that your sermon on Sin will frighten youngsters from one end of the shore to the other.

CATHOLIC JOKES: FATHER DINN ON SIN

FATHER DINN: Well, if Val likes the sermon, I'll go with it. (**FATHER DINN** *stands and starts the sermon on Sin again.*)

And he was taken from that place and cast into the "other place." And there, every part of his body which had offended the Lord burst into flames and burned for eternity.

Good afternoon, boys and girls.

My name is Father Dinn. And I'm here today to talk to you boys and girls about Sin. Father Dinn talking about Sin. Now that was a little joke. I told you a little joke because I'm going to talk to you boys and girls today about *jokes.*

You know, over the years, a lot of boys and girls have asked me, "Father Dinn," they say, "did our Lord tell jokes?" *(Becoming strident:)* Did the saviour of the world laugh at funny stories? Did our Lord have...a sense of humour? *(Then suspiciously calm:)* Of course he had a sense of humour, boys and girls! He was a perfect man.

He had a perfect sense of humour.

But I don't know why it is, boys and girls, *(he's ramping up again; it's scary now)* but for some strange reason or other, I don't think that when our Lord said, "Burn in hell for eternity," that He was joking. I think *that* day our Lord was in...a very serious mood.

Boys and girls, have you ever put your finger on a red-hot stove? Well, I suggest you do. Because the pain of hell is a billion trillion times hotter than any red-hot stove. The pain of hell is no joke.

You know...I couldn't help noticing as I was speaking here this afternoon that one or two of the little boys and little girls *(indicating with his outstretched hand how very small they are)* in grade one, or perhaps even in grade two...are laughing. They probably think *(with growing indignation)* this *whole thing* is a joke! They think: This doesn't matter to *me.* This has nothing to do with *me* because I'm too...*(indicating with his outstretched hand again) little* to go to hell.

(Then with worrisome joviality:) You know, boys and girls, a number of years ago I was very fortunate in having a private audience with our Holy Father, the Pope.

And a funny thing happened on the way to the Vatican.

We were passing through St. Peter's Square when the Holy Father turned to me and said, "Father Dinn," he said, "you know it's a very sad fact, but there are *(heating up) more children under the age of seven suffering the eternal tortures of the damned...(on fire now)* than the human mind can comprehend!"

Yes, it's hard to imagine, boys and girls. Every day, thousands of little souls are sucked careening and swooping into the gaping mouth of

Hell! *(Indicating with his outstretched hand again:)* Little boys and little girls dragged across a hideous bed of broken glass…onto a mound of red-hot coals. *(He mimes the children being dragged.)*

Shrieking for their mommies and daddies who cannot hear them.

For their mommies and daddies are not in Hell, boys and girls… They're in the living room watching television. *(Beat.)* They're watching *The Partridge Family* without you.

No one can help you once you are in Hell, boys and girls. But I can help you now. Before you go to Hell. Because I'm going to give you a special blessing. A blessing which will wipe away all of your sins.

And don't tell me you haven't got any sins, boys and girls, because I heard your confessions this afternoon.

And I was horrified.

More horrified than I have ever been in the thirty-five years that I've been giving this sermon. That's right, boys and girls; I have been giving the SAME SERMON for thirty-five years. *(He begins to unravel.)* In fact, I am *fed up* giving this sermon.

I have had it, boys and girls, up to here.

(Clearly seeing his own mental breakdown, he speaks quietly, calmly:) As a matter of fact, a few moments ago my mind…snapped. *(He snaps his fingers then, quietly, factually reports:)* I'm freaking out, boys and girls. I have flipped my lid. I'm going to go now and jump over the wharf.

(With a new and menacing serenity:) But before I do, I am going to do something that I have always wanted to do. I'm going to show you, boys and girls, my dick. Close the door, please, Sister, lock it up tight.

> **ANDY** *snaps out of* **FATHER DINN** *as the lights start pulsing. He does his mock flashback/freak-out/bad acid trip shtick—with his fingers splayed, he moves his hands in a pulsating movement at the sides of his head.*

ANDY: Wah, wah, wah, wah, wah, wah. Uncle Val writes a letter to Father Dinn. Wah, wah, wah, wah! Father Dinn listens to Reverend Freep's sermon. Wah, wah. All his characters have lives of their own!

Wah, wah. Big freak-out! Wah, wah! *(He stops suddenly, looks at audience suspensefully.)*
   Intermission!

   Blackout.

~ **INTERMISSION** ~

PART TWO

THE AUDIENCE IN MY BEDROOM

ANDY *returns to the stage. He is now fully dressed and is wearing his overcoat as if he has just come indoors. He carries a grocery bag. He behaves differently now. He is alone and seems unaware of the audience. He has the poster for tonight's show in his hands. He places the grocery bag on the table. He opens the poster, stares disgustedly at it, and whimpers with inner disappointment. He throws the poster onto the ground. He is agitated and upset, on the verge of tears. He has a short, silent mimed argument with an imaginary person. He whimpers as he starts to remove his clothing. He is very preoccupied. He strips to his underpants. He heads back to the table but is stopped by catching sight of himself in an imaginary mirror. This "mirror" is in front of the audience, so by looking into it, he looks directly at the audience. He takes stock of his flabby body. Jiggles his belly fat. He tries to do some strong-man muscle-flexing poses. He is disappointed. He flicks his man-boobs with disgust. He grabs a handful of belly fat, sticks the eraser end of a pencil into the middle of the fat, and squeezes it, propelling the pencil out towards the audience. Then he puts a cassette tape into his belly fat and propels that too. He picks up the cassette tape recorder and considers trying to propel that also. He decides not to. Thoroughly depressed now, he goes to the table and takes a jar of peanut butter and cheap unsliced white bread from the grocery bag. His whimpering turns to mild crying as he tears out a large chunk of bread from the middle of the loaf, forms it into a big, doughy ball, scoops out a huge handful of peanut butter, and smears the peanut butter on the bread. Licks the excess off his fingers. Takes a big bite of bread and peanut butter. He walks around, lost again in that imaginary unhappy conversation. Then, in mid-chew, he suddenly notices the audience! He is in shock. They are still here in his room! He swallows the bread and, in a panic, starts speaking to the audience.*

ANDY: Oh, oh my. Uh, welcome back, ladies and gentlemen. *(Trying to look and sound calm, he puts on his clothes very quickly and scrambles to return to the thread of his life story, swallowing his bread and peanut butter as he speaks:)* After I left Newfoundland, I went to Toronto. I worked at Theatre Passe Muraille with a young director by the name of Louis Del Grande. And he's now got his own TV series too! Then I went to England, with the Ken Campbell Roadshow, where I learned to drive the nail up my nose. And where I also learned to set fire to my own head—which I still hope to do later in the show.

(Assisted by pulsating lighting effects, he repeats the flashback/freak-out/bad acid trip shtick with pulsing fingers.) Wah, wah, wah, wah. Actor returns home from theatre; audience is still there. Wah, wah, wah. All the world's a stage. Wah, wah, wah, wah, wah, wah! Freak-out wah, wah!

UNCLE VAL: Calm down, Andy. Calm down. Shur, there's nobody out there, look. Shur look, shur there's a wall there, luh. *(Feeling the invisible fourth wall:)* There. See? Go on to bed now, go on. Get into bed. (VAL *winks knowingly at the audience.)* Atta boy.

That's it, get in there. There you go, look.

"SUCH STUFF AS DREAMS ARE MADE ON," ## BY WILL SHAKESPEARE

In his mild, musical Job's Cove accent, VAL *quotes Prospero in Shakespeare's* The Tempest.

UNCLE VAL:
"You do look, my son, in a moved sort,
As if you were dismay'd. Be cheerful, sir.
Our revels now are ended. These our actors,
As I foretold you, were all spirits, and
Are melted into air, into thin air…
And like this insubstantial pageant faded,
Leave not a rack behind," sir. "We are such stuff

As dreams are made on, and our little life
Is rounded with a sleep."
That's it. Go to sleep. *(UNCLE VAL pulls up the covers, kisses ANDY, who is in the bed, and tucks him in. He then pulls a chair up to the stage left side of the bed.)*
Have you done your pee? All right. Okay, all right, I'll tell you a story. I'll tell you a story. All right, let me see. Um…

JACK MEETS THE CAT: EPISODE ONE

The lighting changes, suggesting an outharbour kitchen lit by oil lamps. VAL speaks quietly—he is used to being heard during the long evenings in the kitchen.

UNCLE VAL: Once upon a time, many, many years ago, long before you were born and long before I was born, and that's a long, long time ago, there was a man and a woman got married and they had three sons. And they called them Tom, Bill, and Jack. Now Tom and Bill, they were kind of handy. They were actually able to do something.

But Jack! Jack was another story altogether. All he ever done was sit around in the coal box all day long. He never washed his face, he never combed his hair, and he never shaved until he was twenty-one years of age. All he ever done was take a potato, stick it on his big toe, stick it in the fire, roast it, and eat it. And that's how Jack spent his time.

Now one day Jack's two brothers, Bill and Tom, they come into the kitchen. They said to their mother, "Mudder," they said, "bake us a cake and roast us a hen, for we're off to seek our fortune."

Well, their mother was crushed. She was broken-hearted at the thought of Bill and Tom—her two bouncing baby boys—going down the road to seek their fortune. But the next day when Jack said to his mother, "Mudder, bake me a cake and roast me a hen, for I'm off to seek *my* fortune," all the mother said was, "Whist ta booneen, Jack. Me prayers have been answered! 'Tis not for your going I'm sorry, 'tis only afraid you'll come back."

"That's the right way too, Mudder," says Jack. You see, Jack and his mother, they never got along all that well. So Jack headed down the road to seek his fortune, and he said to himself, "Today, on me first day seeking me fortune, I'm going to walk for a hundred miles."

So he walked, and he walked, and he kept on walking, he didn't stop walking, he walked some more. He did walk. He did walk. He didn't not walk. He didn't not walk, and he walked, and he walked, and he walked, and he walked, 'til he stopped dead in his tracks. Ninety-nine point nine miles. He couldn't go another step farther. His legs was swollen up like balloons and his feet was falling off the bottom of his legs.

He said to himself, "I think I'll go into the woods and take a little rest."

So he did. *(Scary voice:)* But the trees were very, very tall. It was very, very dark in the woods. And Jack was quite frightened. And all of a sudden, he was set upon by a wild and woolly band of gypsies.

And as was the gypsy custom at that time, they decided to...*(a cliffhanger)* eat him up for their supper!

RICARDO'S ORIGIN STORY, PART TWO: MOM, POP, AND FIERY RED WINE

RICARDO: If I might interrupt, Uncle Val, for one second here. I actually remember the day that Jack was brought into the gypsy camp. Yes, Val referred to us as "wild and woolly" gypsies, but he could not possibly understand.

For we were renegade gypsies. Even the gypsies called us gypsies!

Yes, we went from one gypsy camp to the other, all the way from the toe of Italy right to the crown of Russia. That's why you may notice that my accent slips around a little bit. And my gypsy parents, you ask? Well, sometimes they were kind to me, and sometimes they were cruel. Es la vida, wha?

But I can remember often, *(teary-eyed with nostalgia)* late at night when my gypsy Pop would get drunk on the fiery red gypsy wine, he would stand my mother against the caravan, and he would throw knives at her! And then, later, when they both drank the red wine, they would dress me up as François, the little crippled clown. And I would sing my song *(Singing in emotional Maurice Chevalier style and a French accent):*

Let them laugh, let them smile,
Let them chuckle a while,
(*He laughs a hollow, broken-hearted laugh:*) Ha ha ha!
(*Smiling desperately through his tears:*) I don't care; I'm a clown
I...have...no...heart... (*His face falls with epic sadness.*)

And then the three of us would put our arms around one another, and we would cry our way through the night until the sun, like a boiling peach, rose at dawn...

UNCLE VAL: (*Slightly annoyed and dismissing the melodramatic* **RICARDO**) Thank you very much, Ricardo. That was very interesting.

Um, yes, (*getting back on track*) oh yes, of course. It turned out, as it happened, that Jack was a very good dancer. So the gypsies decided not to eat him for supper because they needed a dancer—because they ate their last one. But, in the meantime, in the neighbouring kingdom of Muldonia, the great king of Muldonia, King Bolognia, was having a birthday party for his beautiful daughter, the Princess Freckelonia. Everyone was there—kings, princes, dukes, earls, big folk, small folk, folk like you folk, and folk like me folk. And who do you think was entertaining the king and the princess that night? Why, Jack and the gypsies!

And, needless to say, Jack was the star of the show. He danced and he danced, and he kept on dancing. He didn't stop dancing, he did dance. He did dance. He didn't not dance. He didn't not dance, and he danced, and he danced 'til his legs was swollen up like balloons and his feet was falling off the bottom of his legs. And all of a sudden, the grand ballroom went right silent. The princess stepped down from her throne. She walked over to Jack and she said,

"Jack, will you dance with me?"

Jack said, "Don't see why not."

And Jack began to dance with the princess. And the orchestra played the most beautiful waltz that ever was heard since the Cherubim Big Band played the music of the spheres.

And Jack fell madly in love with the princess. And the princess fell madly in love with Jack.

But of course, *their love could never be*! For she was a high and mighty princess, and Jack was nothing but a poor and lonely beggar boy. So, sadly, Jack had to say goodbye to the princess, and the princess had to say goodbye to Jack.

Forever.

And Jack, with a heavy heart, headed down the road once again to seek his fortune.

He was walking along for three or four miles when he come to the side of a river, where he sat down and he took off his little swag bag. He opened it up and took out some of the cake his mother had baked for him and a little bit of the hen that she had roasted and a hard-boiled egg. And to tell you the truth, *(miming it:)* a tear come to Jack's eye, rolled down his cheek, and fell into the salt on the top of his egg. Poor Jack. He was feeling pretty low.

When all of a sudden, he seen the strangest thing he ever seen in his life. He seen a canoe. A huge, lugger canoe, with four square sails fore and aft. And rowing in the canoe, there was a…

(**VAL** *looks over at* **ANDY** *in the bed and whispers:*) Oh. He's asleep. He's a funny fella. Ha. He thinks he invented me. And of course, the opposite is true. But I don't mind. We each of us have our tawdry peccadilloes of the psyche.

Good evening, my name is Valentine Reardigan, and I'm your host this evening for *Out of the Bin*.

The patient, to paraphrase the words of the character Treplev in Anton Chekhov's play *The Seagull*, imagines he's working for the cause of humanity. For the "holy cause of art." When to my mind, all he does is display the chaotic ravings of a man who suffered some strange incident during his toilet training.

TENSE UP! (1983 NATIONAL THEATRE SCHOOL TRAINING)

Leaving the **UNCLE VAL** *character,* **ANDY** *takes over again. He repeats the flashback/freak-out/bad acid trip shtick with pulsing fingers. He is assisted by pulsating lighting effects.*

ANDY: Wah, wah, wah. Character takes over actor, wah, wah, wah, who is real in this hall of mirrors? Wah, wah. Wah, wah, wah, wah, wah, wah. Tension! Big heavy-gear tension! National Theatre School–type tension. I am a National Theatre School...AC-TOR! *(Runs athletically across to the opposite side of the stage, stops, sticks out his arms to the side in his rigid "ac-tor" stance.)*

Every muscle in my body tense at all times. National Theatre School actor "Walks"! *(He walks; it is totally studied and rigid, yet somehow, he imitates human movement while tensing every muscle in his body.)* National Theatre School actor "Answers the Telephone." *(Again, he uses every muscle in his body to answer the phone. It's as if he has broken this simple action into ten discrete actions.)* After three years of training, totally incapable of normal human activity but perfectly trained to act in dull and dorky theatre all over the world, where they teach you to bow like this! *(He imitates the look of a famous, beloved—yet humble—actor. He bows ridiculously deeply. He makes an under-the-breath crowd-cheering noise/applause sound.)* With a humble look on your face like you've just saved some child who fell over the wharf, but in fact all you've done is talk in an English accent and dress up in foolish costumes for two hours. *(Repeats the under-the-breath crowd-cheering noise/applause sound, then does the dramatic kettledrums and quirky sound effects of a CBC Radio documentary:)* Boom, boom, boom, boom. Chee, chee.

OIL FOR AMERICA, PART TWO:
WAKE UP, CANADA! AMERICA IS INSIDE YOU

CBC RADIO ANNOUNCER: *Sunday Morning*, a week in the life of the world. Senator Gordon Goodbar's "send them all to Arizona" speech causes shock waves throughout the Canadian political establishment. The Senator retracts.

SENATOR GOODBAR: *(With his American Southern populist accent:)* Well, here I am again. I don't know for the life of me why I am here. But I am here, and here I am. Now I get one little old telephone call from one little old lady in Newfoundland, and being the big teddy bear I am, I go

OUT OF THE BIN • 47

on the radio and try to help you to patch up your shattered dreams of oil prosperity. And now every day I'm getting hundreds of calls from Newfoundland. My second wife, Lola, my one and only sugar pie, said to me, *(with a hint of an imitation of Lola's pretty voice:)* "Gordon," she said, "you are an *American* Senator, you got your own constituency. You are National Vice-President of the Girl Guides of America, Secretary Treasurer of the Moral Majority, you are under indictment for six counts of bribery, and you are leading contender for the Vice-Presidency in 1988. You are a very busy man, Gordon. And if you get involved with those people up there in Newfoundland, I'm going to that cocktail party by myself."

People of Newfoundland, my wife is a very beautiful woman. She is also very, very young. In fact, I met her at a Girl Guide convention. She is an incalculable asset to my political future. If she found out I was even *talkin'* to you tonight, she would chop off my privileges. So I'm going to have to be brief. Now, since I last talked to you, I did a little investigating. I got my secretary, Mary Louise—real nice Northern girl, Mary Louise, real quiet and got real thick glasses—I got her to contact one of your politicians, Mr. Brian Peckford, who happened to be visiting Washington at the time. A very, very pleasant man. A deeply emotional man. A man disturbed…by the issues in his homeland. And he told me the fascinating four-hundred-year history of a simple people in bondage to the sea and the rocky land. Of a people at the mercy of the weather and the times, just like the rest of the world. And so, the next day I flew to your province. That's right. I have been in your country, and I have found it beautiful. And the people, though not conventionally beautiful because they are not as well fed as Americans, are nonetheless *warm* and…*proud* like…*(searching for it)* roosters in the sun. And while I was there, I realized that you people ain't got any problems. *(Turning a bit cruel:)* You never had nothing anyways. And what you did have you blew. You gave away your electricity, you gave away your fish, you gave away your forests, and now sure as shooting you're going to give away that oil. So when you see them bundles of hundred-dollar bills being loaded aboard foreign-going vessels, you just thank the good Lord God that you got jobs loading them!

Like Lola always says to me, after she's had a few dry martinis, *(Lola voice:)* "Gordon," she says, "you were a slave to your pappy. You were a slave to your first wife. And now you are a slave to me. All you ever done was change masters."

And then I cry for a little while. Then she fixes me a drink and says to me, like I'm saying to you, *(a sweeter version of Lola:)* "See, things ain't so bad."

ANDY: *(Again, he does the dramatic kettledrums and sounds of a CBC Radio documentary:)* Boom, boom, boom, boom. Chee-chee.

CBC RADIO ANNOUNCER: In the Senate:

SENATOR GOODBAR: *(Quivering with emotion:)* Mr. Speaker, I hereby declare that I wash my hands of the problems of the people of Newfoundland. *(In a public way to Lola in the visitors' gallery:)* You listen, and you listen good now, Lola. *(Back to the speaker of the Senate:)* And furthermore, Mr. Speaker, I will return all correspondence *from* that place *to* that place! So help me God! *(To Lola in the gallery:)* Are you happy now, Lola?

NEWS FOR STUPID PEOPLE

CBC RADIO ANNOUNCER: Boom, boom, boom, boom. Chee-chee. And now, with the News for Stupid People, here's Andy Jones.

SNOTTY NEWSCASTER: *(As condescending as possible)* Are you listening? *(Calmly, overenunciating as if to a deaf person:)* I'm going to read you the news. *(Rolls his eyes ever so slightly.)* In Iran this morning...Iran! It's a country in the Middle East. Iran! Next to Iraq. Look, *(gestures behind him)* it's up there on the map in big, ignorant letters for you, okay. Iran, right? *(Takes a breath to calm down.)* In Iran this morning, the Ayatollah Khomeini *(stops, disgusted)*...oh Jeezez you'll never get that one, will you. *(As if to a child:)* Okay, he's a very important religious leader...okay...kind of like the pope. *(To himself:)* Well he's not like the pope because he's a political leader too. *(Back to the stupid people:)* Well, he's kind of like the pope and Brian Peckford combined. *(Weary, he starts again.)* In Iran this morning, the pope and Brian Peckford issued a communiqué…issued a *communiqué!* He made a "big statement." *(Giving up:)* Oh, there are a lot of bad things going on in the world, but they got nothing to do with you, okay, so just stay in your houses, shut your windows, close your doors—we…we'll send you food packages in the mail!

Now just turn off your TV and go to bed. *(Frustrated:)* No, turn it off. No. Off. *(Yelling)* No, off! The "off" button! Off! Jeez. *(Sigh of relief—they've gone to bed.)* Now the News for Everyone Else.

CBC RADIO ANNOUNCER: Boom, boom, boom, boom. Chee-chee. And now on Arts Report, our regular feature. From Newfoundland, poet John Formyle with his reflections on a far-flung outpost in a fading empire.

FROZEN STIFF AND SHRIVELLED: SPRING IN NEWFOUNDLAND

JOHN FORMYLE: *(An arrogant, upper-class British expat exiled in Newfoundland)* Thank you. Due to the disgusting nature of Spring in Newfoundland, Marjorie and I make our own Spring. We carry on *just* as we did in England. The first week in April, we have our first planting, which is immediately cut down by ice and snow the second week of April. But then, in the spirit which has made our people what they are—"thin red line," "fight on the beaches," etc.—we stand undaunted and proceed to the *second* planting in the *third* week of April. Peas, usually. *(Aside:)* We've got an interesting strain this year, pre-minted and pre-mushed.

Then, with almost miraculous speed, they are destroyed by frost.

Then at about the time that the daffodils appear in England, I surprise Marjorie—well, it's not a surprise really, because I do it every year—by going down to the local flower shop, if you could call it that, and buying two dozen cut daffs—that's daffodils to you—which I then take home and stick into little holes in the ice. And then I call out to Marjorie, who is in the house with the curtains closed, *(shouting:)* "Marjorie, the daffs are up." (*He laughs, very amused at himself.*) The neighbours must think we're mad—as if I cared. And then, (*snapping his fingers*) before you can say "Bob's your uncle," the daffodils have gone all frozen stiff and black and shrivelled.

And then I go inside the house, and quite frankly, Marjorie and I have a good cry.

This usually leads to Marjorie's "why can't we go back to England" speech, to which I inevitably reply, "Darling, we can't, the people need us here, they simply don't have the local expertise, we must see ourselves as missionaries," etc. This usually brings Marjorie round. This and three or four ounces of gin. Poor Marjorie, she never fitted in, really. But of course, she wanted to. That was her problem. I never cared. She had such potential too. Fifth form field hockey captain, almost head girl, national milk monitor's girl of the year. Anyway, here's my poem. A little light please, John-Paul. (*Special poetry spotlight comes on.*) Thank you.

Spring in Newfoundland.

Oh Spring, oh Spring, oh what a thing
To twangle the aortas of my heart.
Oh, season hidden on New*found*land's hellish isle,
From you I'll never part.
Your British incarnation, however, is as a song, still humming in
  my ear
Even as I sit here, (*begins to sob*) weeping Albion tears into my beer.
Oh, take me away, dear God, from these pine-clad frozen hills
And set me down in Wordsworth's host of daffodils.

(*Pulls himself together.*) The poem isn't finished yet, but I think it's worth working on. This is John Formyle. I'll be back again tomorrow night with my poem on bigotry. Hmmm..."Bigotry," "bigotry." It's so hard to get a word to rhyme with it. "Oh bigotry, oh bigotry..." (*pause; gets it!*) you grow like a fig-a-tree." Ah, there we are. John Formyle, thank you very much, carry on, it's been bags of fun.

OUT OF THE BIN • 51

CBC ANNOUNCER: Boom, boom, boom, boom. Chee-chee. President Reagan cannot conceal his annoyance at Senator Gordon Goodbar's accidental revelation of what turned out to be a top-secret American plan. Code name: The Big Resettlement. The president, however, hotly denies that he called the Senator "a meddlesome idiot" or "subhuman filth." Act Three. From the Senate to the Gutter.

OIL FOR AMERICA, PART THREE:
WE'RE COMIN' TO GET YA, PECKFORD!

SENATOR GOODBAR: *(Walks over and throws himself on the bed in a depressed and drunken state.)* People of Newfoundland, I tried to help you. I tried to help you. *(Then, pushing away imaginary handlers:)* Get away from me! You get, get out of here! Go on!…They're trying to stop me from talking. They're trying to stop me from telling the truth. I ain't a Senator no more, I ain't got an office no more, I ain't chairman of nothing no more, and the president of the United States called me up and said, "You shut up about Newfoundland. You shut up about Newfoundland or I'll tell everyone about your wife."

Well, I don't care. So my wife left me. She left me a note and said, "Gordon, you ain't my teddy bear no more. I'm going to find me a new teddy bear."

Well, I don't care. You hear me, Ronnie? I don't care! I could say a thing or two about his wife at that big party at the White House, but I won't. But I tell you, that lady ain't as stiff as she appears to be. That lady can let loose. Ya-hoo! Oh. *(Suddenly nauseous)* I feel sick. I'm going to have to go to the little boys' room. But before I go, I'm going to tell you something. I've been kicked out of the Senate, I've been convicted on those six counts of bribery, my wife left me, I ain't a Senator no more, and I've been drunk for ten days. But I tell you, I'm thinking, I'm thinking maybe, maybe I should come up to Newfoundland and run in your little election. The president of the United States called me subhuman filth. So I'm going to start my own party in Newfoundland. The American Party of Newfoundland. You hear me, Peckford? I'm coming to get you!

The Americans are coming to get you. If you elect my party, we won't care who owns the offshore because we're getting all the money. If you elect me, after a while we're going to get the bomb. We can nuke the mainland! Then the offshore is ours forever! We can nuke the whole goddamn world! Yahoo! *(Falls asleep in the bed.)*

UNCLE VAL: *(Waking up in the bed.)* Oh, I fell asleep. Oh, oh, Andy's asleep too. Well, I guess in a very real sense, that is my talent! *(In his soft northern Conception Bay accent, he gently mocks* **ANDY***'s "This Is My Talent" fanfare:) Yes.* Bump, pa-bum. Ba, ba, ba, pa-bump, pa-bum. This is *my* talent. I wear salt-and-pepper caps and plaid shirts, thereby fulfilling the National Film Board ideal of the Newfoundland fisherman. Bump, pa-bum. Ba, ba, ba-bump, pa-bum. I tell traditional Newfoundland stories in a pre-dominantly middle-class setting. Bump, pa-bum. Ba, ba, ba-bump, pa-bum. The only thing left now, juxtaposition-wise, would be for me to start using Newfoundland obscenities such as dickey-licker, nob-gobbler, cunny-hopper.

"NOB GOBBLING": OBSCENITY ON THE STAGE

ANDY: *(Cutting in suddenly)* I'd just like to, uh, at this point, say a few words about obscenity on the stage. I sometimes wish when people complained about what they call...*obscenity* on the stage, or when they close films and arts shows and so on, and those shows are called obscene, I wish *that* was the real obscenity of the world. It'd be nice if *they* were the only problems that people were forced to write letters to the editor about. In that case, the real problem in the Middle East would be...like... Yasser Arafat is going out with Shimon Peres's girlfriend.

PALESTINIAN: *(With a Newfoundland accent)* Jesus, Yasser b'y, you know, ask him to the party, ask him to the party.

ARAFAT: No way, b'y. I'm not recognizing any of that Israeli crowd after what he did to Susan.

BRITISH MEMBER OF PARLIAMENT: *(Upper-class British accent)* Mr. Speaker, Mr. Speaker. I move that this house deplore the recent actions of Mrs. Thatcher and Mr. Ronald Reagan, and furthermore state that the British people will not continue to support their illegitimate children.

PARLIAMENTARIANS: Hear, hear! Hear, hear!

MARGARET THATCHER, PRIME MINISTER: *(In her permanently exasperated voice)* Mr. Speaker, Mr. Speaker.

SPEAKER OF THE HOUSE OF COMMONS: The honourable the Prime Minister.

MARGARET THATCHER, PRIME MINISTER: *(She speaks passionately with her very plummy accent. She is lost in love.)* Mr. Speaker, it was a *love* child.

PARLIAMENTARIANS: For shame! Hear, hear!

ANDY: I bet if I was to take this show that I did tonight to Holy Heart of Mary Regional High School for girls in St. John's and say to one of the nuns: "Sister, I have to say 'dickey-licker' in this show," I wouldn't be allowed to do the show. Even though all around Holy Heart, dicks are being licked, nobs are being gobbed, cunnies are being hopped!

Yet I bet I could sing my song.

*(**ANDY** sings:)* I know a guy.

(Speaks aside:) I really do know this guy; he lives in Alberta, he's got red hair.

(Sings again:) I know a guy who knows a gal, who knows a gal,

Whose baby had its brain smashed out

Last week, last week in Central America.

(Singing:) America, America…

(Stops suddenly, mimes picking up the phone:) I'm sorry, Mr. Reagan can't come to the phone right now, he's up Mr. Begin's hole.

MARGARET THATCHER, PRIME MINISTER: (*Passionate, plummy, and impatient*) Mr. Speaker, Mr. Speaker. Due to the increase in homosexuality in the British Isles, good red-blooded British boys can't find any nookie. I therefore propose that we invade the Falkland Islands in search of nookie.

ANDY: (**ANDY** *bum-pa-bum-bums to the tune of "Rule, Britannia!":*) Bum, pa bum bum, pa bum pa bum pa bum...Nine months later in the House of Lords...

BRITISH LORD: (*Crusty old Brit codger*) My Lord Chancellor, Mrs. Thatcher's precipitous actions in the Falkland Islands have resulted in fifty illegitimate British births. And worse than that, my Lord, thirty-eight of them are Welsh!

GENERIC LIVE COVERAGE ANNOUNCER: Mr. and Mrs. Chernenko attended the grand ballroom. She was wearing a pink chiffon dress, and the chairman of the Communist party was wearing a green chemise and...nothing else. Good night.

MÉNAGE À SEPT

UNCLE VAL *sits on the side of the bed.*

UNCLE VAL: (*Speaking to* **ANDY**, *who is presumably in the bed:*) Oh no, I'm not saying good night to *you.* What? Oh, yes, of course. Yes, of course, that would be the ultimate juxtaposition: if I were to get in bed with you—thereby implying that you're having a homosexual affair with one of your own characters. I love it! And yes, they'll love that in Denmark. Yes, excellent idea. (*Gets in bed, pulls the covers up.*)

> **ANDY** *reaches up and mimes turning off an overhead light. Blackout. We are in darkness. All the characters from the show are in bed together.*

FATHER DINN: Good evening, Uncle Val.

UNCLE VAL: Father Dinn, what are you doing here?

FATHER DINN: Good question.

REVEREND FREEP: Would you please be quiet, I'm trying to sleep.

UNCLE VAL: Reverend Freep, you're here too.

REVEREND FREEP: Yes, we're all here, for some bizarre reason or other.

SENATOR GOODBAR: And I'm here too. I don't know for the life of me why I'm here, but I am here and here I am.

RICARDO: Senator Gordon Goodbar with your strange accent, I think I know why you are here. You are here apparently to put your cold feet all over me! Kindly remove them!

JOHN FORMYLE: All right, who farted? And this is not a case of "The Donkey Who Dealt It Smelt It."

RICARDO: Mister John Formyle with your beautiful English accent. I find it amazing to think that you could possibly smell a fart, you, who have at the bottom of your legs the most stinking feet in the history of human endeavour. (*Suddenly having a heartburn recurrence:*) Ah. Ah, shit. (*He burps loudly.*)

JOHN FORMYLE: Aha! I knew it was you.

RICARDO: No, it wasn't me, it was the green slimes I ate for my dinner today.

REVEREND FREEP: (*Making orgasmic masturbatory sounds:*) Ah, ah, ah, ah…

UNCLE VAL: Reverend Freep! Stop that.

REVEREND FREEP: Ah, ah. Ah. *(He stops.)* Oh, I'm sorry. An abominable habit. Well, tell us the story then. Finish the story for us, Uncle Val.

UNCLE VAL: All right, I'll finish the story for you. And by the way, where's Jones?

ANDY: *(Does the flashback/freakout/bad acid trip sound effect. It is supported by a very low-level pulsing lighting effect:)* Wah, wah, wah, wah.

JACK MEETS THE CAT: EPISODE TWO

UNCLE VAL: Calm down, for God's sake, Andy, calm down. All right, I'll just light the candle here and finish the story. *(Strikes match, candle fails to light.)* Perhaps I'll have to mime lighting the candle. Oh yes, here we are. *(Stage lighting fills the room.)* What a lot of light for a mimed candle. Now, where was I in my story? Oh yes, of course. Jack had just sat down by the side of a river. And he seen a great big lugger canoe coming down the river with four square sails fore and aft. And rowing in the canoe there was a cat. "Hello, Jack," says the cat.

"Hello, puss," says Jack *(surprised that a cat is talking to him)*.

"What are you doing?" says the cat.

"Well," says Jack, "I'm looking for a master."

"Well met," says the cat, "because I'm looking for a man. Will you ship to me?"

"Well," says Jack, "'tis as well to ship to you as ship to anyone else, shur."

And so Jack got aboard the canoe and he stayed with the cat for a year and a day. And every morning Jack got up and scrubbed up the canoe from stem to stern. Every day he brought the cat breakfast in bed. And they had a wonderful year and a day together.

But when the year and the day was almost over, Jack and the cat were sitting in the canoe one day, and who do you think they seen going home through the woods but Jack's two brothers, Bill and Tom, with great big bags of money on their backs. And each of them also had a beautiful woman by the hand. Well, when Jack seen that he was vicious. He said, "Look at that! There's Bill and Tom gone home with beautiful women by the hand, and what do I got after a whole year and a day? Nuttin' but an old cat."

Jack got himself into an awful bad mood, and every time the cat spoke to Jack, Jack would only grumble.

And after a while, the cat said, "Uh, Jack, you seem to be in an awfully bad mood."

And Jack said, (mocking the cat's tone:) "No, I'm not in an awfully bad mood."

And the cat said, "Yes, you are in a bad mood."

And Jack said, "No, I'm not in a bad mood."

And the cat said, "Yes, you are in a bad mood."

"No, I'm not in a bad mood."

"Yes, you are."

"No, I'm not."

"Yes, you are."

"No, I'm not."

Finally, Jack broke down and he told the cat what was on his mind. The cat says, "Well, well, well. Was that what you wanted, Jack, a woman to take home by the hand?"

"Yes, of course," says Jack.

"No problem," says the cat.

And the cat reaches into her pocket, and she takes out the one half of a ring. And she hands the half a ring to Jack, and she says, "Jack, when you find the woman who has the other half of that ring, guaranteed she will be the woman of your dreams."

"Thank you very much," says Jack.

"And now," says the cat, "Today is the twelve-month and tomorrow is the day, but before I give you your money, before you go, I want you to do three things for me."

"No problem," says Jack.

"Number one," says the cat, "go out in the woods and get me a great big pile of dry wood." Jack goes out in the woods and gets a great big pile of dry wood.

"Number two," says the cat, "take that dry wood and build me a great big roaring fire." Jack takes the dry wood and builds a great big roaring fire.

"Number three," says the cat, "I want you, Jack, to throw me into that fire."

"No," says Jack, "I could never do that."

"Yes," says the cat. *(With great authority:)* "I am your master, and you are my man. Now do as I say."

"No," says Jack *(adamant)*, "I'll never do that!"

"Yes," says the cat *(angry)*, "you've got to do that!"

"No," says Jack, "I'll never do that!"

"Yes," says the cat, "you've got to do that!"

"No," says Jack, "I'll never do that!!!"

"Yes," says the cat, "you've got to do that!!!"

And after a while, Jack loses his temper, picks up the cat and throws her in the fire! *(Makes scalded cat sound.)* Well, the cat bursts into flames, shoots up through the chimney, and disappears.

Jack says, *(with a horrified look)* "Oh no! What am I after doing? I'm after killing the cat. I'm going to jail for the rest of me life and I'll be hung for murder!"

When all of a sudden, a knock comes onto the door!

Jack goes over and opens the door, and standing at the door is the most beautiful woman that water ever wet or the sun ever shined on. It was the princess. The Princess Freckelonia, from the neighbouring kingdom of Muldonia. Jack says, "Princess, what are you doing here?"

She says, "I come to see you, Jack."

And Jack says, "You couldn't a'come at a worse time."

"Why is that?" says the princess. And then Jack tells the princess the story of how he killed the cat.

The princess says, "After all, Jack, the cat did *ask* you to throw her into the fire."

"I know," says Jack. "But that's no excuse for killing a cat."

Then the princess says, "Jack, uh, by any chance…did the cat give you anything before she burst into flames?"

And Jack says, "Yes, as a matter of fact, she gave me this one half of a ring." And what do you know but the princess reaches into her pocket and takes out the other half. And the two halves fits tight together.

Jack says, "Princess, you are the woman of my dreams."

And she says, "Jack, you are the man of my dreams. Now we can get married," says the princess.

"Yes, yes, yes," says Jack.

"And live happily ever after," says the princess.

"Yes, yes, yes," says Jack. *(Sudden tragic change:)* "No, no, no," says Jack. "I forgot. I'm after killing the cat. I'm gunna go to jail for the rest of my life and be hung for murder."

Then, all of a sudden, the princess says, "Jack, don't worry about the cat."

"Don't worry about the cat?" says Jack.

"No," says the princess, "the cat is not dead."

"The cat is not dead?" says Jack.

"No," says the princess, "I am the cat."

"You are the cat?" says Jack.

"Yes," says the princess, "I was turned into a cat by an evil wizard. And he told me that I would be a cat forever unless I could get a man to serve me, as a cat, aboard a canoe, for a year and a day, and throw me into a fire! And you done it, Jack. You saved me from eternal catdom."

Jack says, "But what happened when I threw you in the fire?"

"Well," says the princess, "I burst into flame, shot up through the chimney, up through the clouds, up through the sky, all the way to heaven. Then an angel come along in a blue jumpsuit and a tennis racquet and boinked me *(mimes a tennis racquet boinking downwards)* right back down to earth again. As soon as I landed on the ground, I was a princess once again!"

"Well," says Jack, "come on home and meet me mudder."

He takes the princess by the hand, takes the bag of money over his shoulder, goes over hill, down dale, up meadow, across bridge, over underpass, under overpass, bottom line, ballpark figure, up the front path, in through the kitchen door, and…who do you think is standing there waiting for him? His mudder.

She don't see Jack, she don't see the princess. All she sees is the bag of money. And the eyes is bulging out of her head. (*Once again,* **ANDY** *makes his eyes bulge by putting his glasses in the flesh under his eyes.*) And Jack takes the bag of money and slaps it down on the floor. But the bag busts, and the money goes all over the floor. And the old woman goes nuts trying to pick the money up, trying to pick the money up, trying to pick the money up. So Jack comes along and gives her a puck of his knee and drives her under the table. She don't mind that, she keeps on trying to pick the money up, trying to pick the money up, trying to pick the money up. So Jack comes along and gives her another puck. But this time she struck her head against the hob of the fireplace, and with that the racket riz.

"I'll bet," says Jack's father from the other room, "Jack is home."

Well, after a while Jack and the princess, they told the mother the story of how the princess had been turned into a cat. And guess what? It turned out that two other young women who went home with Bill and Tom, well, they were the princess's two younger sisters. And guess what again? Later that year, the old king, King Bolognia, of Muldonia, he retired. And he made Jack and the princess King and Queen of Newfoundland and Labrador. Yep. They were crowned in an elaborate coronation and marriage ceremony that took place right here at the LSPU Hall at St. John's. Everyone was there, everyone. Ricardo was there, now the Secretary-General of the United Nations. John Formyle was there—the poet laureate of the new kingdom. Father Dinn was there; he performed the marriage ceremony, and it went something like this:

HELLO, SHACKLES! HELLO CHAINS!—
FATHER DINN ON MARRIAGE

FATHER DINN: And when I say, "Do you take this man, do you take this woman," I mean do you take those days when you sit across from one another at the breakfast table and you say, "Good morning, hon," and you really mean…"I hate you." And when your spouse turns around, you actually mouth the words. *(He mouths the words "I hate you.")*

I mean do you take those days when you meet one another coming out of the bathroom, and you say, "Hello darling," and you really mean hello shackles, hello chains, hello agonizing, bone-grinding torture of my life—are you finished in the bathroom? I mean do you take those days when you stand helplessly by while you watch your little thirteen-year-old daughter tart herself up for some cheap dance at Holy Heart of Mary Regional High School? Or when you're looking for your little boy, your former bundle of joy, your little Billy or Tommy or Bobby—and where is he? He's out in the back yard talking about getting a few scrapes. I mean do you take those days when you say, "Dear Lord Jesus, come down off the cross—take the nails out of your hands and feet, dear Jesus—you can do it if anyone can—and get me out of this flaming holocaust called marriage." If you do, then say "I do."

TIN BED BENDS; STORY ENDS

UNCLE VAL: Well, needless to say, Jack and Princess said, "I do." And after the ceremony was over, they had a wonderful big banquet. Everyone was there, yes, Margaret Thatcher was there with Mrs. Gandhi—her new lover! Yasser Arafat, Shimon Peres and Susan were all there—now living in a ménage à trois. Mr. and Mrs. Chernenko were there in matching pink chiffon dresses. And everyone had a wonderful time. And Ricardo that night declared it World Peace through Nookie Year. And when the dinner was over, they all got together in a great big tin bed. But the tin bed bended, so my story's ended. If the bed had been stronger, my story would have been longer. And if they don't have good luck, then may all of ye. Good night. *(He blows out the candle.)*

Blackout.

Out of the Bin was first presented at the LSPU Hall, St. John's, Newfoundland and Labrador, on Friday, June 17 and Saturday, June 18, 1983, under the title *All his old material is... Out of the Bin—Andy Jones performs his greatest hits from the past.*

Friday's show was a benefit for Mary-Lynn Bernard's volunteer stint with Canadian Crossroads International in Guyana; Saturday's show was for the benefit of Andy Jones! The show was co-produced with the Resource Centre for the Arts. Showtime was 8:30. Admission was $3.00.

Performed by **ANDY JONES**
Direction and dramaturgy by **CHARLIE TOMLINSON**
Script written by **ANDY JONES**
Additional material from:

1. the folktale "Jack Ships to a Cat" as told by **PIUS POWER SR.** and adapted by the **SHEILA'S BRUSH THEATRE COMPANY**, including **FRANK BARRY, GEOFF PANTING, AGNES WALSH, MERCEDES BARRY, PHILIP DINN**, and **ANDY JONES**. That original production was assisted by **VAL RYAN, ANITA BEST, FLIP JANES, ELLY COHEN, DAVE PANTING, LLOYD BEST, MARK OAKLEY, FRANÇOIS CAMBRON, DELLA COHEN, BILL BARRY, VICKI HAMMOND**, and **BRIAN BEST**

2. the "Arizona Proposal" sections of the play *A Midsummer's Nightmare* by the **SHEILA'S BRUSH THEATRE COMPANY**

3. the "Nail up the Nose" from *An Evening with Sylvester McCoy, Human Bomb*, by the **KEN CAMPBELL ROADSHOW**

4. Prospero's speech from *The Tempest*, by William Shakespeare.

Lighting design and operation **FLIP JANES**
Pyrotechnics **KENT BARRETT**
Set, props, and costumes **ANDY JONES, CHARLIE TOMLINSON**
Original poster design **TIM PECKHAM**

And thanks for anecdotes and inspiration from Mary-Lynn Bernard, Mary Walsh, Michael Jones Sr., Agnes (Dobbin) Jones, Sheila's Brush Theatre Company, Anita Best, Pius Power Jr., and the entire Power family from South East Bight and Clattice Harbour Southwest.

TOURING HISTORY

In June 1983, Andy Jones wrote and opened *Out of the Bin* at the LSPU Hall in St. John's, Newfoundland. It was co-produced by the Resource Centre for the Arts. It ran for two nights: Friday, June 17 and Saturday, June 18, 1983.

It was then held over and ran for six nights at the LSPU Hall: Tuesday, July 5 through Sunday, July 10, 1983.

In the fall of 1984, Andy toured *Out of the Bin* to Ontario, playing at Theatre Passe Muraille in Toronto, the Great Canadian Theatre Company in Ottawa, and Kam Theatre Lab in Thunder Bay.

As a benefit for the LSPU Hall renovations campaign, *Out of the Bin* was reprised at the LSPU Hall from January 16–20, 1985. In June of that same year, it played at the *Festival de théâtre des Amériques* in Montreal, Quebec.

From January 18–21, 1995, excerpts from *Out of the Bin* were presented in Calgary's One Yellow Rabbit's High Performance Rodeo. Under the title *Oral Comedy*, this production also featured excerpts from Andy Jones's show *Still Alive*.

PRODUCTION NOTES

Every production of *Out of the Bin* used the material that is contained in this book. Variations in the performances were minor. The transcript of the show in this book was based on the 1984 performances at Theatre Passe Muraille, Toronto, and on a videotape of an earlier performance between January 16 and 20, 1985—videotaped in St. John's by Mike Jones, with sound by Jim Rillie.

Since *Out of the Bin* had a comparatively short life, Andy Jones reprised a number of the show's sketches and monologues later in his five other one-man shows.

Props, Costumes, and Set Pieces

Costumes, Part One: striped pyjama top and soccer shorts.

Costumes, Part Two: Jockey shorts, winter coat, winter slip-on boots, socks, button-up shirt, and slacks.

Props and set pieces: large outdoor metal garbage bin; single bed; bedside table; two wooden chairs; a sturdy table with a chair suitable for the sit-down "lecture on comedy"; box of chocolates; piles of newspapers and magazines; large Raggedy Andy doll; patterned quilt; blankets; pillows; takeout cups; "big boss" Pepsi bottle; Crispy Crunch and Big Turk chocolate bar wrappers; an empty used Kentucky Fried Chicken bucket; used pizza boxes; various crumpled chip bags; one large empty chip bag; dirty socks; various shirts, pants, stale foodstuffs; large can of rolling tobacco; cigarette rolling papers; a poorly made prop rat (piece of fluff pulled offstage by a string); matches/lighter; working plug-in clock radio; one roll of toilet paper; writing paper; pens; small box of Tetley tea bags; a mug; a plug-in electric kettle filled with cold water; an extension cord; one large sticky bun; small tub of margarine; butter knife; hammer; one two-and-a-half-inch nail; a bottle of Dettol; one piece of cotton batting; tiny knitted baby's mitten; tiny pair of doll's shorts; flashlight; a small cassette tape recorder and a cassette tape; a grocery bag containing a jar of peanut butter and a loaf of cheap, unsliced white bread; a poster from the show that is being performed; a pair of eyeglasses; a candle; a pile of white cardboard signs (each card says one of the following: "ANDY JONES"; "COMEDIAN"; "ELEVEN"; "F@#K"; "AND CALLED ME

DUSTY"); four piles of index cards (each card says one of the following: "Elements of Humour Cards"; "Snappy Patter"; "Juxtaposition"; "Wit"; "Infuriating Humour"; "Guess The Canadian Town"; "Edu-Cards"; and "Personal Confessions").

KING O' FUN
(A LEAP O' FAITH)
by Andy Jones

TABLE OF CONTENTS

A catalogue of the one-person sketches, bits, reflections, and comedy routines contained in *King o' Fun*, a stage show during which two parallel dimensions attempt to connect.

Crucial Cheeseburger, Part One: Fish and Chip Formula 70
"Whizgigging"—What Does It Mean? 71
Fish Tank Philosophy 72
Slipping into the Whizgiggian Dimension 72
The Burden of the Comedy Crown 74
"Meaning of Life" Hats 74
Crucial Cheeseburger, Part Two: The Fatal Flower 75
Plato and Aristotle As If They Were Newfoundlanders 76
How I Was Crowned King o' Fun 80
Oil on the Breasts 81
The Rooster Bishop of Borino 82
More Oil on Those Breasts 86

Crucial Cheeseburger, Part Three: Rescue Mission 87
Chekhov: Everything He Ever Wrote—In Three Pages 88
The Overacting Gene 92
Crucial Cheeseburger, Part Four: The Wheel of Perpetual Striving 94
How the Whizgiggians Wear Their Pants 94
Gander Syndrome 96
The Funniest Human Being in the World 98
A Dog Named Antidisestablishmentarianism 99
Germs with Heart Conditions 99
Sweet-Talking My Bowels 100
Ilya's Voice-Activated Prosthetic Leg 101
Half-Dog 103
Funerals For Arnold Schwarzenegger's Victims 104
Boiling Oil on Robin Hood's Not-So-Merry Men 104
Irish Lament 106
Crucial Cheeseburger, Part Five: The Comedians' Entrance 106
The One-Man Square Dance 107
Funniest Human in the World Arrives 109
Calling on God/Giving Up on God 112
Crucial Cheeseburger, Part Six: They Are Coming to Get Me 112
King o' Fun: Final Report to the World 114

ANDY JONES'S NOTES ON *KING O' FUN*

Like *Out of the Bin*, this show is pretty much a "shaggy shapeless series of sketches"—but this time I added a plot!

This plot develops from evidence that the show is being observed by people from a parallel dimension called Whizgiggan. In fact, there is reason to believe that I was born in that dimension—where I was a handsome, charismatic, king-like figure.

Unfortunately, I fell to earth and became myself.

But tonight, during this particular shaggy, shapeless presentation, evidence will emerge that the people of that other dimension are trying to rescue me and bring me home before the show ends.

And that, my friends, is the plot.

Am I rescued? Do I return to the Whizgiggian dimension?

Read on, sensation seekers!

And please, no whispering, giggling or suppressed laughter meant to annoy, especially old people.

—AJ, December 2023

Dramatis Personae:

ANDY—*a human being. He is a comedian who plays several characters in his one-man live theatre show* King o' Fun, *which is being presented in the human dimension.*

JORELLO ANDISBRÖTTIR—*a Whizgiggian being. He is an earnest television news anchor and public affairs analyst who is simultaneously presenting TV coverage of* **ANDY**'s *theatre show to the people of the Whizgiggian dimension.*

DARLENE—*a human being. Assistant stage manager for Andy Jones's human dimension theatre show.*

The Time: Right now

The Setting: There are two coexisting dimensions—the human dimension, where **ANDY** *presents his one-man show entitled* King o' Fun, *and the Whizgiggian dimension, which simultaneously presents the same show as part of Whizgiggian TV's constant coverage of everything* **ANDY** *does.*

*   **ANDY**'s *stage is practically empty, except for a few items upstage left. They include an open suitcase, a chair, and a metal garbage can.*

In the centre there is a 20-foot by 20-foot canvas floor cloth. Painted on this floor cloth is a large circle; inside the circle is a Mayan-style image of a man suppressing a laugh by holding his hand over his mouth. This circle serves as a portal between the two dimensions.

There is a white screen on the upstage wall.

The lighting, sound, and video effects tell us immediately which dimension we are in.

CRUCIAL CHEESEBURGER, PART ONE: FISH AND CHIP FORMULA

"Telstar" by the Tornados plays loudly as **JORELLO** *is beamed down and stands in the eerie light that indicates the Whizgiggian dimension. He is standing in the centre of the circle that is the portal between the two dimensions.*

JORELLO: *(With the serious, self-important, educational tone of live television reporting)* When the human beings say "You are what you eat," they are right. What they don't realize is that there is a crucial moment when they can start to *become one food.*

For example, our scientists speculate that upon eating the critical 1,911th fish and chips, a human being of approximately one hundred and fifty pounds starts to *become* fish and chips—because at that moment a majority of their cells have been encoded with fish and chip "memory cravings"; the cells then metastasize and begin to take over the entire organism. Yes, the irreversible march has begun!

Only shortness of human lifespan prevents that person from literally *becoming that foodstuff,* sitting there on a cardboard container with salt, vinegar, and tartar sauce, so *(pointing to the following formula on the screen:* "$H^\infty \times F(1,911) = F^1$"*)*

H, or human, to the power of infinity, times F (or foodstuff) to the power of 1,911 *equals* F to the power of 1 or...the foodstuff...in this case fish and chips.

STRANGE AUDIENCE MEMBER: *(Mildly aggressive)* But have you ever proven it by seeing a human being turned into a foodstuff?

JORELLO: *(Flustered)* That is completely beside the point. The point is that the process has begun—and it cannot be undone! But yes…we have, through the use of human stem cells and a cyclotron, managed to turn a human into fish and chips. *(Annoyed:)* But in any event this is not a question-and-answer format!

Ladies and gentlemen, we now return to our twenty-four-hour live coverage of An-dee and everything he ever does. *(On the screen, a Whizgiggian TV standard graphic says "24-hour Live Coverage of An-dee and…everything he ever does.")*

As you know, at this very moment, he's performing his one-man show *King o' Fun* at the LSPU Hall in St. John's and he's about *(looks at watch)* let me see, the show went up about two minutes late…he's about twelve minutes into his show…*(There is a dramatic end-of-show kettledrum sound effect as part of the Whizgiggian TV show. We now enter the human dimension. The Whizgiggian TV lights fade, and we enter the full, warm light of the human world.* **ANDY** *is doing his show. He too is standing in the middle of the circle. There is a huge "canned laughter" sound effect.* **ANDY** *enjoys this laughter immensely. He is very pleased with himself.)*

"WHIZGIGGING"—WHAT DOES IT MEAN?

Our audience has no idea what has caused this laughter. From the open suitcase, **ANDY** *picks up a cheeseburger in his left hand; canned laughter increases as he threatens to eat it. He stops himself from taking a bite by exaggeratedly pushing his left arm away with his right hand; he repeats this gesture twice. Each time, joyous canned laughter accompanies the move. Why are they finding this funny? We don't know.* **ANDY** *then gives up and puts the uneaten cheeseburger into the suitcase.*

ANDY: Anyway, that word appears in the *Dictionary of Newfoundland English*. The word "whizgigging"—it's the Newfoundland word for that kind of conspiratorial laughter that children might do at the dinner table, like…*(He whizgiggs—an explosive laugh, inadequately repressed by his hand over his mouth.)* "Stop your whizgiggin' and eat your supper!" *(A* *graphic appears on the upstage wall showing the phonetic symbols of the word "whizgigging," as well as the* Dictionary 'of Newfoundland English *definition. He points to the wall graphic.)* Here's the entry in the *Dictionary.*

(After the phonetic symbols, the graphic on the screen says: "Whizgigging— whispering and giggling in such a way as to annoy, especially old people." Then he takes a copy of the Dictionary of Newfoundland English *out of the suitcase and shows it to the audience.)*

This is the *Dictionary of Newfoundland English*...great book...*(Ad libs his praise for the book.)*

(Beat.)

FISH TANK PHILOSOPHY

ANDY: *Our* scientists speculate that each time a fish decides to change direction, all reality starts again for him. He has no memory of anything previous to that decision, and then, by the time he gets to the other side of the fish tank, he's even forgotten his decision to go there. So I figure it's like this for fish in a fish tank. *(He goes from a distracted, unfocused look to dramatically noticing the opposite side of the stage:)* "Wow! There's another side to this tank." *(He crosses enthusiastically, stops, forgets why he was going there, accidentally looks back in the direction he just came from, is shocked:)* Hey! There's another side to this tank. *(He crosses, stops, forgets, accidentally looks back in the direction he just came from, is again equally shocked:)* Hey, there's another side to this tank! *(He crosses again, stops, forgets, accidentally looks back in the direction he just came from—yet again he is equally shocked:)* Hey there's another side to this tank! *(Repeat to taste.)*

SLIPPING INTO THE WHIZGIGGIAN DIMENSION

I do that sometimes, just to see if I can come up with some new material: I walk in one direction *(he does so)*, turn around *(he pivots)*, and start again! That's how I came up with this idea that there is a *dimension* called Whizgiggan—a dimension right next to ours *(mimes a wall very close to his right side)*, and when you're a kid doin' that *(he whizgiggs—laughing explosively while trying to repress it with his hand over his mouth)*, it's like, at that moment, *everything human* seems so utterly ridiculous that the curtain between the two dimensions *(he mimes parting curtains on his right)* opens up for just a second and you could eeeeeasily just slip into Whizgiggan and be lost forever. *(He moves right, as if he has slipped into the other dimension.)* It's like human existence really is a joke and at that moment *(he whizgiggs again)* you *get the joke*, freeing you to travel anywhere in time and space. But children can only laugh like that in the presence of authority, and authority always brings them back before they go too far. The example in the *Dictionary of Newfoundland English* is "Stop that whizgigging, you'll be crying the once." *(On the screen, a graphic shows the* Dictionary of Newfoundland English *entry saying: "Stop that whizgigging, you'll be crying the once.")*

And that laughter always does seem to end in tears. It's like you laugh at the great joke of human existence and then immediately you're heartbroken because...well, human existence is a joke. And of course, once you're an adult you can never *ever* laugh quite like that again...

And I was walking around thinking about this, and I turned *(he pivots like the fish in the tank)*, and I had this *idea* that in this other dimension, where everything's pretty well perfect, where all problems are pretty well solved and where death does not exist—*they're trying to get in touch with me!*

I went to CBC with the idea—I mean, for a TV series based on it. In the show, I'd be me, Andy Jones, St. John's actor, my family would be my family, my house'd be my house—so it'd be cheap—like those reality TV shows.

Only what I don't realize (me, this guy in the TV show) is that back in the Whizgiggian dimension, I'm "An-dee," their greatest and noblest leader; I'm their Nelson Mandela, their Winston Churchill, or I'm Atticus from *To Kill a Mockingbird*.

Remember in the courtroom scene in the movie of *To Kill a Mockingbird*, all the black people are up in the balcony and all of a sudden, they all stand up, and the little girl—Scout is her name—she asks the guy, "Why are you standing?" and the guy says *(pointing down, as if from balcony)*, "We're standing up cause your father is passing by."

Whoa! I'm *that* guy, in that other dimension. And also, he's played by Gregory Peck, so I kinda look like Gregory Peck in the other dimension except that...(*He runs to suitcase.*) fifty-seven years before this—back in the Whizgiggian dimension—I accidentally touched the petals of *this* enchanted flower (*picks an artificial but very realistic rose from the suitcase*), which caused me to fall to earth, forget who I am, be born as a human baby, and grow up to be...me, Andy Jones, the guy on Gower Street, the guy in the TV series...(*Somewhat at a loss:*) And, well, that's the whole idea. (*Pause; he's a bit disappointed in his own idea.*)

CBC didn't like the idea either. But I never stopped thinking about it.

THE BURDEN OF THE COMEDY CROWN

ANDY: (*Still holding on to the enchanted flower*) But like I was tellin' you during the first twelve minutes of the show, these are the kinda notions that have been going through my head in the last year and a day since I was crowned King o' Fun. (**ANDY** *puts on a well-constructed but homemade crown from the suitcase. The lights dim for a second.*)

And I wanna make it clear that *that's what I'm doin' here*—passing on fun notions that have come my way in the past year and a day. I mean, that's what I'm doing here on *this* stage. I don't mean "that's what I'm doin' here on this earth"—passing on fun notions that have come my way—(*he laughs nervously*) obviously I've got more important things to do than *that* with my life. (*His useless life flashes before his eyes for a brief second; he recovers.*)

"MEANING OF LIFE" HATS

ANDY: For example, like this Bulgarian guy came up to me at a restaurant in St. John's the other day and told me about "Meaning of Life" hats. I don't know if you've ever heard of those, but apparently in this small district of Bulgaria called Gooseneckia, all citizens are required by a very ancient custom to go into the woods by themselves for six months, during their adolescence, to design and *make* a hat which they think best explains what we are doing here upon this earth. 'Course, each person keeps working on their hat all their life, and once a year all citizens who have completed their hats gather in the town square and then, in a loud voice and all together, everyone *explains their hat*. Then they stop and wait, hoping that the meaning of life will become clear, to all of them—all at once. And, of course, every year there's a groan of disappointment; they take off their hats. (**ANDY** *takes off crown, holds it in his hand, places it on top of dictionary—but he holds on to his rose.*) And everyone trudges sadly home. Of course, some people say the whole thing is just a way of getting rid of their adolescent kids for six months.

CRUCIAL CHEESEBURGER, PART TWO:
THE FATAL FLOWER

"Telstar" music theme; the lighting transforms the stage into the Whizgiggian dimension.

JORELLO: *(Standing in the middle of the circular floor graphic portal)* Here he is: An-dee. Human. Once he roamed the endless happy meadows of Whizgiggan; he shared in the hard-won perfection of our dimension—then through (some would say) no fault of his own, he touched the petals of this flower, *(holding on to the stem so that the flower does not touch him)* the petals that no Whizgiggian must touch. This has become our *central event*, the defining moment of our culture for the past forty-nine years and the reason you are watching this twenty-four-hour live coverage of *An-dee aaaaand everything he ever does!*

(On the screen there is a Whizgiggian TV graphic saying: "24-hour Live Coverage of An-dee and…everything he ever does.") Why, in our nearly perfect world, did we lose our brightest, our bravest, our handsomest, our most charismatic warrior-lover, artist-scientist leader…and to *this* human incarnation? Miserable, food-obsessed, and confused. Oddly, after our massive efforts and the expenditure of billions of gek-geks of our hard-earned money, we seem to have only slightly nudged his life in such a way that he became an actor, then a sort of comedian; then he wrote this one

comedy sketch in which we appear as foolish fictional characters. *(He goes into poetic commentator rhythms:)* Oh, how do we reverse the effect of the petals? How do we reach through the curtain *(he reaches out to his side with his left hand)* and pull him back home once again? And, as you know, the cheeseburger in his suitcase will be his 1,347th.

It is the Crucial Cheeseburger!

As soon as one molecule of that foodstuff passes his lips, it will render him a hopeless candidate for reintegration into the purity of our dimension. Yes, fellow Whizgiggians, we are probably only hours away from the final failure of our rescue mission. The countdown continues...

> *There is a sadder, more muted version of the TV show's kettledrum effect—with a hint of impending doom. The lights transform into the human dimension, where* **ANDY** *is performing in King o' Fun. The canned laughter is rising and falling. Again,* **ANDY** *is enjoying it. He has obviously just finished a long speech ending in a laugh. He too holds the flower in his hand.)*

ANDY: Anyway, my point is: The flower is important, don't forget the flower! (**ANDY**, *making a spooky* oooohhhh *comedy sound, brings the flower to touch his nose. There is more canned laughter. There is a dramatic electric shock noise, a moment of puzzlement on his face, a toilet flushing sound, it's a joke—he laughs at the whole idea of the flower; he places the flower on the right side of the suitcase—petal end towards the audience.)*

It's another one of those fun notions that have come to me in the past year and a day, I guess as a direct result of being crowned King o' Fun... *(He picks up the crown from inside the suitcase but does not put it on.)*

PLATO AND ARISTOTLE AS IF
THEY WERE NEWFOUNDLANDERS

ANDY: ...Anyway, like I was saying during *(he is in a slight trance)* the first twelve minutes of the show, I said: "Yeah, Danny"—this is Danny Williams, he's the head of the cable company in St. John's so I figured he'd understand—"Yeah, Danny, to answer your question I *am* suggesting we try to be all things to all people. This…is about everything, yeah, I know I am biting off more than I can chew, yeah, I am trying to swallow the whole hockey puck; so what?

"I keep telling you, Danny, we don't have to be like anything else that's gone before…there is nothing else like what we've got here in Newfoundland and Labrador In. The. World! So let's tell our stories; they are among the great stories of the human race. I want us to produce shows…ten, twenty, fifty shows! The answer is to go deeper into the rainforest to find new plants, new cures for the ills of humanity!"

I was so inspired for those few moments, standing there in Danny's office with my King o' Fun crown on *(he puts on the crown)* and my Whizgiggian flower in my hand—it was all still new to me—I'd only been the King for about two weeks at this point—and besides, CBC and Geoff Stirling had just turned me down for the Whizgiggian show. (I thought for sure Geoff'd go for it!) But it turned out Danny said yes.

No, not to the Whizgiggian show idea *(he takes off the crown, holds it)* but to a series called I*fffff*. Did you see it? It was a show where every famous historical character was presented as if he'd been a Newfoundlander. This was the opening sting.

> *Theme music and video graphics on the upstage screen play a low-tech standard TV opening montage: it starts off with the word* Iffffff, *then dissolves to a series of shots of famous people with* **ANDY***'s face superimposed on their faces: Che Guevara in his hat, Napoleon Bonaparte, a hockey hero holding up the Stanley Cup, Charlie Chaplin as the Tramp with the little boy, St. Patrick, John Cabot, and Jesus.)*

ANDY: Like, one week we did Plato and Aristotle as if they'd been Newfoundlanders; the scene takes place in a bar, in Athens around 500 BC. (**ANDY** *puts the crown and the flower back in the suitcase and gets the chair and sets it centre stage.)* Aristotle is sitting here having a quiet drink. *(Goes to the suitcase and gets a Greek laurel–type crown.)*

ANDY *as Plato stumbles in loaded. There is subtle sitcom opening music with Greek bouzouki flavour.* ANDY *walks towards the chair.*

PLATO: *(Obviously drunk and belligerent, he slurs his St. John's–accented speech.)* Question-and-answer time. Why did Plato cross the road? *(Silence.)* Why did Plato cross the road? *(He has frightened everyone in the room.)* I said, "Why did Plato cross the road?" *(He walks to the chair woozily miming grabbing Aristotle's shirt and talking right up in his face.)* 'Cause he wanted to kick the shit out of Aristotle!

ANDY *sits; he becomes Aristotle, grabbing his own shirt front.*

ARISTOTLE: *(Unfazed by having his shirt pulled by Plato, he takes a sip of his beer, puts it down on the table, then looks up coolly at Plato, who stands over him:)* Pack off, Plato b'y, you're drunk.

PLATO: *(Standing:)* No! NO!!! Aristotle, I am not drunk...you are *sober!* *(Thinks he is quite clever. Then with a low menacing drunken laugh:)* Write that down! Somebody write that down! They'll be quoting that 3,000 years from now. I am the greatest philosopher in Greece today! And come ahead anyone who disagrees!

ANDY *performs Plato being suddenly grabbed by the hair—*ANDY *grabs his own hair—and puts one hand behind his back as if being handcuffed; then he mimes being dragged off, as he yells.*

PLATO: What the fu...get your hands offa me. Jeez, the cops...People of Greece, rise up! The philosopher Plato is about to be thrown into the drunk tank! *(Pause. No response.)* I said rise up!...Ye sons a bitches. What is this, Ontario? Ye little shits. *(Whining, crying:)* Ow, ow ow, these handcuffs are hurtin' me hands, b'ys. *(He exits;* ANDY *runs back to chair and becomes Aristotle.)*

ARISTOTLE: *(Quietly)* Jeez, b'ys, Plato's losing it. He's becomin' his own absolute drunk, the *essence* of drunkenness. *(He likes the idea and writes it*

KING O' FUN • 79

down.) I like that. *(There is a standard TV "wah-wah" sitcom passage-of-time sting done with bouzouki.)*

ANDY AS NARRATOR: The next evening, Aristotle is in his usual chair when Plato returns...

PLATO: *(Obviously sobered up and contrite)* Good evening b'ys. *(Rubbing his hands)* I'd like to say I'm sorry for my behaviour last night. *(Swallowing his pride:)* And I'm particularly sorry for what I said to you, Aristotle. *(Reaches down his hand to shake it with the sitting Aristotle.)*

ARISTOTLE: *(Beer mug in left hand, he reaches up to shake Plato's hand.)* Don't worry, Plato my son, it's all grist for the mill...

PLATO: *(Disdainfully)* Yes, I'm sure it is, Aristotle. Anyway, by way of recompense, I'd like to buy a round for the house *(Fudahhowss)*—on me. No, no need to applaud...the only reward I seek is a little philosophical banter! *(Mimes taking a beer off a tray.)* Tank you, Mavis. What's that? Question-and-answer format? Good idea, Gerry. You've all met my younger brother Gerry. Gerry Plato. He's in ladies' lingerie. Hahahaha. Only kiddin', Ger. He's a lingerie salesman. Okay, hit me Ger. *(Listens to Gerry's question, throws it back at him:)*...What are we doin' here??!! Woohoo!! Oh, oh, ya mean what are we doin' *here*? I thought you meant *(Big quotes; looks towards the heavens:)* "WHAT ARE WE DOIN' HERE" *(Beat.)* Oh, ya did! Cut to the chase, why don't ya, Ger!...Any theories, anybody? *(Closing sitcom music with Greek flavour sneaks under* **ANDY**.*)* Anybody got a hat that might explain it...*(Plato finds this funny.)*...only jokin', Andy...Ye all know my cousin Andy Jones visitin' here from the future. *(Sitcom show music begins to fade as Plato says a trail-off line:)* Now if I was gunna make a hat, I'd do it democratically...

Like a music conductor, **ANDY** *conducts the lights and music as they fade from the ancient Greek bar world.)*

ANDY: That's it. Plato and Aristotle. *(He bows. He puts Plato's laurel wreath downstage of the suitcase and walks towards the audience.)*

Well, in the end it turned out it was every great historical figure, not so much as if he was a Newfoundlander, but as if he was that one townie *(i.e., St. John's)* character that I always do, so it didn't work out all that well.

But the important thing for me was that the Quest had begun. And I was determined, as long as I wore the crown, I would not go down into the depths of despair that I was telling you about during the first twelve minutes of the show. *(Places the crown on the chair.)* No more standing in front of the open fridge door in the middle of the night eating cheese and crying, crying and eating cheese, eating cheese and crying *(walks to suitcase, takes out cheeseburger)*; no more of the stress-induced eating that I was telling you about *(repeats the "almost putting it into his mouth" gesture from the beginning of the show)*. From now on, light-light-light! Pure fun! Just searching for logs of lightheartedness floating on the river of life. *(Puts the cheeseburger back in the suitcase. Walks across the stage in "story" mode.)*

HOW I WAS CROWNED KING O' FUN

ANDY: I should tell you the whole story. Well, it happened exactly a year and a day ago today. I was here in St. John's, looking for a performance space for my one-man show *Out of the Bin* in this theatre. Quite late in the evening, I came here to this hall to have a look.

When I got here, there were a bunch of construction workers. They were doing some repairs to the ceiling over there. At least they were supposed to be. In fact, they were quite drunk.

And you know that feeling you get when you're cold sober and you walk in at the high point of someone else's drunken party, and you know that with their special drunken radar they can see that you're miserable and they're determined to cheer you up at any cost…

Anyway, between the jigs and the reels, these construction workers end up taking this crown that they'd made, and one of the construction workers—this really big scary guy—puts the crown on my head and declares me as "King o' Fun for a Year and a Day."

They find this very funny. But I wasn't really in the mood, so I took off the crown and slipped out the door and went back to my hotel room.

But I couldn't sleep. I keep thinking this coronation had some cosmic significance. That it meant something.

So I come back to the theatre. The construction workers are still here. But they say they have no memory of any coronation! And, at first, I think I've imagined the whole thing, so I turn to go, but as I turn, I see it: THE CROWN. *(He goes over to the suitcase and picks up the crown, walks back to his chair.)* So I pick it up, I put it on, and I address the crowd. I say, "Yeah, it's easy for you—" *(on the verge of tears; full of self-pity)* "you get to have a sense of humour; I gotta be a *comedian*, I gotta squeeze the last drops from the lemon of comic technique!" *(More self-pity:)* "You get to tell jokes, I got to...work on verb placement—where it goes in the sentence."

When I have to go to rehearsals—to put in another day's "funny work"—I gotta lift my legs like this. *(He does his leg-lifting lazzi, wherein he reaches his hands down, clamps both sides of his calves and strains to lift one heavy leg; then he lifts the other; then he lifts the first one again—it takes an enormous effort.)* I gotta get up in the middle of the night and eat cheese by the half-pound! *(He's crying foolishly now.)* Like I told ya before—crying and eating cheese, crying and eating cheese. Poor funny old me. *(He's sobbing)* I was so lonely doing a one-man show I had to ask the stage manager to get me a little cricket so I'd have someone to talk to backstage—*(he brightens up)* but *that* I did find mildly amusing, so I decided I would wear the crown! And it seemed to give me the strength to carry out my foolish mission.

OIL ON THE BREASTS

ANDY: And I guess I was giving off this aura, because people started coming up to me with stories and tips of worldwide fun events. So I decided to leave St. John's and travel around the world—but I only get as far as Gander, Newfoundland, the "Crossroads of the World"... to the Albatross Hotel, when I met this old guy in the bar, and he told me exactly one hundred and one stories—every one of which involved a situation in which he was called upon to help a beautiful woman to remove oil from her breasts.

(As a heavily West Country Newfoundland-accented skipper in a bar) All right, Mr. Jones, story number seventy-four. *Goldilocks's Mudder and the Three Bears.* Then Goldilocks, remember Goldilocks, old Goldilocks, you know. Well, old Goldilocks's mudder comes back to apologize to the three bears on her daughter's behalf, but the bears is out again. And I dunno if it's genetic but she has ta start rootin' around in the cupboards—like mudder, like daughter, wha? And she accidentally upends this lovely cool bottle of virgin olive oil and whatever way she was standin' by the cupboard—the oil goes all over her breasts. It sunk in deep. She had one of dem Swiss maiden's dresses on, like the ones they got at the chicken place only without de blouse. But anyway, the oil sunk in and I 'appens by—the bears' 'ouse was jus' outsida Clarenville—they were Newfoundland black bears owned a house there—and wit' de pitifullest look she turns to me an' says, "If them bears knows I was at their stuff, they'll kill me for sure! So, kind sir, could you 'elp me get this oil offa my breasts?"!!! *(He giggles with delight.)* And Jean-Paul Sartre says there is no God...

THE ROOSTER BISHOP OF BORINO

ANDY: So now things are starting to happen. There must be something to this coronation. The very next morning, still at the Albatross Hotel in Gander, I got a call from the Papal Trivia Support Group in Italy, who felt that in my new role as King o' Fun, I should hear immediately about the "Amazing Rooster Who Became a Bishop." *(Gregorian chant begins in background as* **ANDY** *moves the chair away from centre stage.)*

This is a true story. And I went to Italy to check it out.

In the autumn of 1995, the bishop of Borino, Italy, the Reverend Angelo Sarto, started carrying a small hand puppet in the shape of a rooster to all church ceremonies. The little rooster was also dressed as a bishop, a mini-bishop if you will, with rooster-sized bishop's hat, staff, and tiny brocade vestments with holes cut out for his bushy rooster's tail and trembling red wattles. I've a little puppet here that's sort of like it. *(Goes to suitcase, takes off crown, and puts rooster-bishop puppet on his hand.)* This is not the actual puppet, of course, but it is one similar to it; I'll just join in here. **(ANDY** *puts on his own matching bishop's mitre; the little puppet helps him.)*

At first, the little rooster bishop seemed to be a humble assistant to the bishop of Borino, but then his role grew. His fellow clergy were shocked and concerned; his parishioners, however, were fascinated, and children for miles around filled the church to bursting every day. And since collection plates overflowed, no one bothered to tell the pope. But soon enough, the rooster moved on from being a humble assistant to the bishop and started preaching in place of the bishop. In fact...here is a rare recording of this strange phenomenon; *(to the technician in the booth:)* can we play that, Geoff?

> *A pre-recorded tape plays. It has the ambience of an old recording in a large cathedral.*

RECORDING OF THE ROOSTER BISHOP'S ACTUAL VOICE: *(A high-pitched but comprehensible squawk)* Cock-a-doodle-doo! Sanctissimi populi. Quid est egleesia? Quid est? Missa? Populi? Curia ad Roma? No, no, no, no...

ANDY: Isn't that amazing? That's the actual voice. *(Gregorian chant begins again.)*

Soon the little puppet bishop moved on from preaching to celebrate Mass, ordain priests, perform weddings and baptisms, and hear confessions. Word soon got to Rome.

The bishop of Borino was called on the carpet by John Paul II. A deputation of cardinals held a secret ecclesiastical trial, the transcripts of which formed the basis of a theatrical performance by the Borino Players called *Episcopo Cocké Est—Hey!* Which, roughly translated, means "Our Bishop Is a Rooster...Whaaat?" And if you like, I'll do a scene from that play. They have given me permission to perform it.

The setting is the Sistine Chapel. The bishop of Borino speaks:

Sistine Chapel lighting

BISHOP OF BORINO: *(In a gravelly, slow Eastern European accent)* Eminent cardinals, this little rooster bishop who is always at my side...*(The little puppet interrupts enthusiastically in a high-pitched voice)*

ROOSTER BISHOP: Cock-a-doodle-doo! Hello, Princes of the church!!! Hahaha...

BISHOP OF BORINO: *(Gently)* Be quiet, Bruno.

ANDY: There is much laughter from the cardinals.

BISHOP OF BORINO: *(Serious)* As I was saying, Your Eminences, this little bishop who is always at my side came to me a few years ago a *broken rooster*, his faith lost. Alcohol had drained away his spirit, stories of wicked abusive priests had soured his faith, he had resigned his bishopric and wanted to take his own life. I took him in as my coadjutor bishop, and he began to grow as a human being once again.

ROOSTER BISHOP: That's right. He said it! I'm the human being, he's the dummy! Cock-a-doodle-doo!

ANDY: There is now uncontrollable laughter from the cardinals. They are totally charmed by the little rooster. Then the pope speaks.

ACTOR POPE: *(Terribly bent over; in a slurred voice, thick accent, and hiding the rooster puppet behind his back:)* But can a confession heard by a *puppet* wipe away sins? Is baptism by a *puppet* true baptism?

ANDY: An argumentative cardinal speaks up.

ARGUMENTATIVE CARDINAL: But Holiness, the puppet is held in the hand of a legitimately consecrated bishop.

ANDY: The room bursts into ecclesiastical babble. The rooster speaks up...

ROOSTER BISHOP: Cock-a-doodle-doo! No! *I'm* the legitimate bishop.

ANDY: More laughter from the cardinals; they are bursting now. The pope speaks.

ACTOR POPE: Stop! (*Dramatic pause*) We. Will. Deliberate!

ANDY: And deliberate they did, for nearly twelve years, the question "Can the holy sacraments administered by a puppet on the hand of a legitimately consecrated bishop be real in the eyes of God?" For, by now, fourteen priests had been ordained by the rooster puppet; thousands of confessions had been heard. With improper forgiveness by a rooster, did souls now languish in hell for eternity?

The answer? Let's let the last scene of the play tell us. The pope, the bishop of Borino, and the rooster bishop all appear at midnight on the pope's balcony in St. Peter's Square. The pope turns to the puppet.

ACTOR POPE: (*Bent over and in his slurred voice*) You can make the announcement, my little rooster friend.

ROOSTER BISHOP: (*Squawking*) People of Rome, people of Borino, People of the World—guess what? I'm legit! I'm legit! (*In a singsong/ sing along voice:*) I'm a consecrated bishop of the holy Roman Church! Cock-a-doodle-doo.

ACTOR POPE: (*Exactly echoing the same singsong/singalong cadences but with his gravelly voice*) He's a consecrated bishop of the holy Roman Church! Cock-a-doodle-doo.

> *There is the sound of the crowds in St. Peter's Square bursting into cheers; echoes of* Shoes of the Fisherman.

ANDY: Loud cheers go up from the Square below.

ROOSTER BISHOP: In fact, I'd like to officially announce—I'm running for pope!

ACTOR POPE: *(Very, very emotional and still bent over)* Tears of admiration and affection for our holy rooster friend flow now from our eyes. *(In phony Italian:)* Por sanctissime cocké lagrimae traxeunt. *(The pope loudly kisses the little puppet three times on the cheeks.* **ANDY** *continues chanting in the pope's voice as he puts the mitre back in the suitcase:)* Por sanctissime cocké lagrimae traxeunt.

(Then the pope suddenly exclaims angrily and assertively:) And in the matter of African Catholics being allowed to use condoms: the answer is No! *(The rooster beats the pope over the head for a real Punch-and-Judy comedy ending.)* Ow! Ow! Ow!

ROOSTER BISHOP: That's not the way to do it!

ANDY: *(He pivots and, in imitation of the fish in the tank, intones)* I think I'll go to…the other side of the stage! *(He pivots again.)*

MORE OIL ON THOSE BREASTS

SKIPPER: I was in the Middle East, your Holiness, workin' on the oil rigs. And one day, the old Sheikh comes out with five of his wives to inspect the drill, and whaddya know, while they're standing there…well, she blows! It's a gusher, sir! There's oil all over everything. Me and the five wives runs for the same shelter. *(Enjoying this detail:)* Now whatever way they was standin'…the oil went all over their breasts, and they looks at me with these sad eyes. All I can see is their eyes—they got them veils on *(he mimes the veils under their eyes)*—and they say, "Can you help us get this oil off our breasts!"

And Plato's younger brother Gerry wants to know what we are doing here on this earth!

On the screen there is a quick flash of a slide of Pope John Paul II throwing his hands up and laughing. **ANDY,** *as* **SKIPPER,** *whizgiggs with great delight—which, of course, allows the other dimension to intrude. "Telstar" theme music and strobe lighting indicate that we are moving to the Whizgiggian dimension.*

CRUCIAL CHEESEBURGER, PART THREE: RESCUE MISSION

JORELLO: *(Standing on the portal, in the eerie light that indicates the Whizgiggian dimension)* "Oil on her breasts." *(He is disappointed.)* Ours not to judge. So, our coverage continues...we Whizgiggians are the most advanced creatures in all of the Universes—at least that's what we tell ourselves. Uh-oh, am I about to speak heresy here? Am I about to say that there are beings who are superior to us? No.

There are only two other species in all the Universes who have actually gotten to the point of dispensing with their own bodies—and we are the only ones to have voluntarily brought ours back. And personally, I'm glad we did. But we have paid dearly for this advance, for once again we are susceptible to the petals of that enchanted little flower: Humana Reductio Simplex. And, once in the human sphere, death comes even to Whizgiggians. With An-dee we are attempting to make our very first rescue from the human sphere, and our progress has been astounding: we manage to walk among the humans; our camera crews record every moment of their lives; tourists by the busload gawk at the most intimate of human activities. Why, here I stand giving you a live television report on the LSPU Hall Theatre Stage, centimetres away from An-dee, and still there is no contact.

"Heartbreaking," some would say. "A waste of money," say others. "Let's withdraw now," say others still. What do you think we should do, An-dee?

STRANGE AUDIENCE MEMBER: *(Calling from the back of the theatre)* He can't hear you!

JORELLO: I know that! (*Stressed*) Do you think I don't know that?! (*He's at his wit's end.*) I'm sorry. Ladies and gentlemen, we now return to our live twenty-four-hour coverage of An-dee aaaaand everything he ever does...

> *On the screen we see the graphic "24-hour Live Coverage of An-dee and...everything he ever does" and we hear the dramatic kettledrums as we transition to the human sphere once again.* **ANDY** *has obviously been telling us more about the* **ROOSTER BISHOP OF BORINO** *during* **JORELLO**'s *speech.*

ANDY: That's right! The "Rooster Who Became a Bishop." It's a true story. Although fiction would seem stranger.

CHEKHOV: EVERYTHING HE EVER WROTE—IN THREE PAGES

ANDY: By now I'm receiving so many calls I am forced to take a trip around Europe. First to Russia, to the broken-down remains of a Soviet Union think tank, dedicated to taking all pre-revolutionary Russian literature and discrediting it by proving that it could be reduced to a few essential pages. The think tank was in ruins, but on the floor, I found a faded script which read *The Works of Anton Chekhov in Three Pages*—indeed, I felt it might be the Script of All Russian Drama in Three Pages. It's called *Shebnayakov Days*. With your kind permission, I will perform it for you. (*Crosses the stage and mutters as he gets into place:*) First time in North America...The characters are Elena Halfya, Frigor Potempkinovich Shebnayakov, Alexander Potempkinovich Shebnayakov (brother to Frigor), Torn Ligachev (a doctor), Maria Potempkinovna Raskolnikov, née Shebnayakov (sister to Frigor and Alexander) and Firma, a very, very, old servant...That's very confusing, I know—but the only *really important thing to know* is that Frigor is madly in love with Elena. The play takes place in the living room of the Shebnayakov estate.

Elena, in the middle of a story...

ELENA: *(Sweet and gentle voiced)* And when she took off the mask…it was my own mother! Hahahahahaha!

ANDY: All laugh except Frigor—Frigor:

FRIGOR: *(Agitated)* Mother! Mother! Mother? Mother? Mother! Mother? Mothermothermothermother. Can't we ever forget about them? I'm forty-nine years old; my mother has been dead for thirty years, and yet every day I think of her.

ANDY: —Torn Ligachev:

TORN LIGACHEV: *(Calm and sensible—unlike Frigor)* Well, after all, my dear Frigor…one's mother and one's father…

ANDY: —Frigor:

FRIGOR: Stop! Father! Don't mention Father to me. The man is still alive—he still drives me to distraction every day!

ANDY: Then Alexander—holding out a bottle of valerian drops…

ALEXANDER: *(Calmly, as if soothing a difficult patient)* Please Frigor, calm down—have some valerian.

ANDY: —Frigor:

FRIGOR: Ah! Fathers, mothers, and now look who's giving me valerian—my brother—ha! I defy *anyone* to escape this…bugaboo that is one's siblings. Oh yes, mothers, fathers, brothers, sisters, then of course there's death, the death of this one, the death of that one, and finally one's own death.

ANDY: —Maria: interrupting…

MARIA: Frigor, PLEEEASE!!!

ANDY: —Frigor:

FRIGOR: Oh it's *pleeeeease*, is it? So it's *words* you throw at me—a lifetime paved with the cobblestones of words *(seeing the following words written in the air:)*…"the"…"chair"…ah, ah…*(searching for another random word)* ah, "incontestability, follicle"…"aptitude, wilderness"…"steel rod"—here, let me apply words directly to my skull.

ANDY: *(Acting out what he describes)* He tears pages out of a dictionary, puts them into a bowl, pours water from a jug into the bowl. He then pulls out the wet paper, squishes it up, and applies it to his head.

FRIGOR: A "word poultice"—a word poultice…to draw meaning out of me.

ANDY: And then suddenly on his knees to Elena. *(On his knees,* **ANDY** *starts hobbling frantically across the stage, talking to what must be* **ELENA** *running away from him.)*

FRIGOR: Oh yes, Elena, I'm frightfully, madly, wildly attracted to you. *(He has a radical mood shift; he leaps up—some outside force is obviously controlling him.)* Oh, oh, dance steps (**ANDY** *as Frigor, possessed, dances a crude jig and laughs maniacally.)* Hahahahahaha. We forgot dance steps, didn't we? *(It's a worrisome, over-the-edge laugh. As he laughs, he points exaggeratedly at his own laughing mouth.)* And laughter. We forgot laughter, didn't we? Hahahahahaha—and what comes after laughter—inevitably…yes!!! Large drops of water falling from the eyes. Yes, yes, yes, yes! Tears! Tears, yes, tears—mother, father, sister, brother, laughter, dance, death, and tears. And all before breakfast. And later! We! Will! Go! To! Moscow! I promise you. Though there is no need to go. We have everything we need right here. In fact, I'm going to board up the doors! Firma! Firma, get me some long boards and some stout nails. I'm going to board up the doors.

MARIA: *(Pleading with him)* No, Frigor, no! Leave it as a metaphor please, you'll ruin the walls.

ANDY: Suddenly following Elena around on his knees...*(ANDY does so.)*

FRIGOR: Elena, surrounded by adoring men sick with love for you, nauseous with love, bilious, seasick with love. Tell me, Elena, is adoration wrong?

ANDY: —Elena: *(ANDY quickly stands.)*

ELENA: Yes!

ANDY: —Frigor: *(ANDY quickly kneels.)*

FRIGOR: Yes, it is wrong!!!!

ANDY: —Elena: *(ANDY quickly stands.)*

ELENA: No!

ANDY: —Frigor: *(ANDY quickly kneels.)*

FRIGOR: What?

ANDY: —Elena: *(ANDY quickly stands.)*

ELENA: Yes, I will marry you!

ANDY: —Frigor: *(ANDY quickly kneels.)*

FRIGOR: *(Standing as he speaks)* What? Did you hear that, everyone? Elena's going to marry me.

ANDY: Suddenly Elena pulls out a gun from her purse. She waves it around. (**ANDY** *mimes* **ELENA** *doing so.*)

FRIGOR: Elena, what are you doing?

ANDY: She puts it to her head. Everyone gasps. (**ANDY** *mimes holding gun to his own head.*)
She pulls the trigger. (**ANDY** makes gunshot sound.)
Blackout! (Blackout and simultaneous gasp from **ANDY**.)

THE OVERACTING GENE

ANDY: It was only fitting, after coming from that rich vein of theatrical tradition in Russia, to go to Britain, where science and the theatre had come together...(*Suddenly* **ANDY** *is channelling the fish in the fish tank. He crosses the stage.*) Something's calling me, calling me to the other side of the stage! (*He pivots, goes back again.*) The other side of the stage looks pretty good! (*He crosses the stage again and speaks in an intense documentary-reporter tone with mimed microphone.*)

INTENSE DOCUMENTARY NARRATOR: Hello, this is Andy Jones reporting. Have you ever watched a stage show, a soap opera, or a British movie and wondered "How can they get away with this blatant bombastic overacting?" Well, for a long time scientists believed that overacting was viral, was passed on, actor to actor—from a sneeze, a kiss, or from wearing the costume of someone who had previously overacted in the same role. But now, British scientists working on the Human Genome Project believe that they have isolated the "overacting gene"—that *overacting may run in families*, that only by sterilizing certain actors might we wipe this plague out forever. But hang on, that's a little extreme, you might think; well, so do a lot of actors whose close work with scientists has led to the discovery of "acting gaskets" in the human brain which seal in various human brain liquids and which if overtaxed can be dislodged.

Yes, that's right, it's possible to "blow an acting gasket."

Many older actors and some younger ones who seem to have had a stroke or who shout incoherently at the audience or wander aimlessly about the stage with wild, rolling eyes may be the innocent victims of a blown acting gasket. Pharmaceutical labs throughout the country are rushing to find a medication to control but unfortunately *never to cure* this deadly genetic disorder. *(He drops the documentary narrator character.)*

ANDY: I actually have drawings of the blown acting gasket. Wanna see 'em? You can see here. *(He gets three eleven- by seventeen-inch cardboard panels from the suitcase. [See drawings p. 179] He shows panel #1, in which a crudely drawn actor with a sword at his side is gesturing madly—the intensity of his overacting is expressed by the radiating lines coming off his body. In a cartoon bubble, he is saying "Give me your sword, you swine!")*

Short bursts of overacting can be therapeutic—they contain the seeds of their own cure—providing an explosive release which serves to calm the actor. But here we see *prolonged* overacting: *(He shows panel #2, in which the same actor is now kneeling and holding his sword horizontally in both hands; the radiating "overacting lines" are increased in number and in length. His face is much more frantic now. In this cartoon bubble, he is saying, "I will lift the sword of mine enemy and blah blah blah!")*

Every muscle in the body is tense. Even some muscles which have never been used before are twitching, which can lead to *blowing an acting gasket*—which then leads to a buildup of hot brain liquids which can burst out the side of the skull—as we see in the next picture. *(He shows panel #3, a close-up of the actor's head and shoulders. His ridiculous face has been invaded by his own rolling, googly eyes, and the side of his head is exploding outward, spewing brain liquids.)*

(Afterthought:) This looks a bit like Elmo from *Sesame Street*. Elmo with hot brain liquids bursting out of his head could be the big thing next Christmas...

CRUCIAL CHEESEBURGER, PART FOUR: THE WHEEL OF PERPETUAL STRIVING

As the house lights fade, the "Telstar" theme rises. This time it is played in a jazzier style. We are in the Whizgiggian dimension. **JORELLO** *is beamed down onto the floor canvas at centre stage.*

JORELLO: "Hot brain liquids": this is our great leader now…

Why can't we get through? *(Obviously frustrated)* We who think we are so advanced. Not to worry. Even their own God can't get through to them. When he created them, he cheated himself of that possibility because he created beings who depend for their very existence on their ignorance of their own meaning. A brilliant young god, he created the perfect invention: creatures who long with every fibre of their being to know if there is an intelligence, a plan, a structure, an answer, but who, at the same time, are utterly incapable of finding it. He has invented the wheel of perpetual striving, and this striving and seeking is what keeps them going; this is their species' protective armour—their claw, their fang—if you will.

It's as if he allowed them to figure out the notion of vision but failed to tell them that they have no eyes. Only empty sockets moist with tears for their loved ones who have disappeared into that realm they call "death."

Sound and lights bring us back to the human dimension. There is robust canned laughter. **ANDY** *is enjoying this laughter.*

HOW THE WHIZGIGGIANS WEAR THEIR PANTS

ANDY: Like I was saying, I always figure the Whizgiggians are the same as we are; they are the same species, really. We could mate with them if we could get through. However, there is *one difference* between humans and Whizgiggians: something happened along the evolutionary trail.

And the difference is the way the Whizgiggians wear their pants—they don't put their legs down *into* the material; it's just laid in front, and the pants are held on by a belt. Here, I'll show you. *(Takes off his pants and puts them over the front of his legs—the pants are held up by his belt, which bypasses the back belt loops and wraps around his waist.)* This is how to tell the difference between a human and a Whizgiggian. So, from the front you think "human being." *(He faces the audience. His pants lie against the front of his legs and therefore appear to be worn on his legs.)* But from the side, you realize: Whizgiggian! *(He turns around to reveal the pants are just in front of his bare legs. From the rear view, his underpants are on display.)*

Whizgiggian women wear their skirts on the front like that too. And also, the bottom parts of their dresses—so you can see their underpants. And, of course, everyone knows the answer to the question "What does a Whizgiggian Scotsman wear under his kilt?" And my idea was, at the end of every episode of the Whizgiggian TV series as the credits roll, one of the characters—a different one each week—would always be laughing to himself: *(He laughs a deep and genuine laugh)* "Hahahahaha," and another character would say, "What are you laughing at?" and he'd say "I was just thinking...about the way...*(barely containing his laughter)* the humans wear their pants! Hahahahaha!" *(In a relaxed way,* **ANDY** *walks around the stage, bouncing his pant legs off the front of his legs.)*

I walk around the house like this myself sometimes. I seriously suggest that you try this at home tonight. It's a freeing feeling—sometimes, late at night, if I'm worrying about the lives of movie stars or something, I'll just walk around like that.

But to get the full benefit of the concept, I'm gonna ask Darlene—our assistant stage manager—to show you a Whizgiggian bride. The music's the same... *(We hear the standard wedding march.)*

> *As the wedding march plays,* **DARLENE** *enters downstage centre in a wedding dress with bouquet and veil. She carries her wedding dress train to one side in the crook of her arm. Facing the audience, she continues walking downstage, looking perfectly normal; then she turns her back to the audience, revealing that her skirt is only on the front. We therefore see her underwear. She walks upstage and stops, as if in front of the priest.* **ANDY** *joins her; they link arms and stand still for a moment,*

giving the audience a rear view of their underpants and bare legs. The music fades as **ANDY** *and* **DARLENE** *walk a few steps downstage.*

ANDY: Now, I know the question that's on everyone's lips: "What about the train?" Are the Whizgiggians denied that pleasure? No! Darlene, demonstrate please!

As the recessional music fills the theatre, **DARLENE** *takes the train of the dress, which she has held in the crook of her arm, and, from the front, throws it between her legs—under the front-skirt—onto the ground behind her. It becomes a "train" without obscuring her underwear. Without turning around, she throws her bouquet into the audience and exits.*

ANDY: Why do I think like this? (**ANDY** *puts his pants back on.*) How am I able to put up with these intrusive Whizgiggian thoughts that have been plaguing me ever since I was crowned as King o' Fun? It's like I have Whizgiggian Syndrome, but, like I was telling you during the first twelve minutes of the show...

GANDER SYNDROME

ANDY: I've been so susceptible in the last year and a day. I even had Gander Syndrome this year. Are you familiar with that? It's a disease where you think you're in Gander even when you're not; there's been no attempt to find a cure, 'cause it's not really that serious. The only symptoms are you keep wanting to go to the Albatross Hotel for a beer, or wanna go for a spin as far as the airport. If you live *in* Gander, it's no problem at all. You don't even know you got it. And if you don't live in Gander, you're always thinking: My God, Gander has changed! If you're in Toronto, you think: My God, Gander's got a subway! I'm not sure if going to Gander once makes you immune, like you build up antibodies, or if you catch it from going to Gander, and it remains latent in your system forever...

So these things made me freer. The thought that I'm this handsome hero in another dimension, and living with the wonder, the awe, of the constant changes in Gander. These things made me more receptive to interesting things all around the world, and it's then that I began hearing rumours about the Funniest Human Being in the World.

THE FUNNIEST HUMAN BEING IN THE WORLD

ANDY: I actually went to Germany, where he or she was last seen. Now apparently, the Funny One walks into serious, real-life human situations and does this "funny act." People report laughing as they have never ever laughed before.

The Funny One, or "Das Liebe-Tiklin," as he is called in Germany, hits like lightning, no one knows where next, and no one has *ever* gotten *any* documentation—up to this point. Well, actually there is one blurry picture of an exiting foot. (*On the screen we see a blurry picture of a glimpse of a person's leg just as they run offstage.*)

So, I arrived in Stuttgart, Germany, and I think I may have caught the last few seconds of one of his funny events. Unfortunately, by the time I got my tape recorder on, I could only capture the laughter. Could I hear that laughter, Geoff? (*We hear the recorded sound of uncontrollable laughter.*) The tape recorder doesn't do it justice—and I can't describe the laughter. It was childlike laughter. But not whizgigging. It's more what the older Newfoundlanders would call *hobbyin'*, the kind of laughter that makes your head go back and forth (*he demonstrates*) like a hobby horse. The example in the *Dictionary of Newfoundland English* would probably be: "stop your hobbyin', you'll be cryin' the once." That's all I managed to get. The laughter. Just the laughter. I later spoke to a German woman who had been there, and she described him to me.

GERMAN WOMAN: (*In a thick, precise, monotonous German accent*) Yes, I can describe him to you. Half of him vas painted blue; the other half vas white. In place of his own nose, he vas wearing a pig's nose. He was wearing *half* of a white, fluffy Hitler-style moustache, but white and fluffy you know. For a hat he was wearing a shell, his foot vas stuck in a bucket und he was saying something frightening, then doing this: *(He raises his arms to cry out angrily to God:)* Aaaaaaargheeee!

ANDY: Her husband concurred...

SECOND GERMAN CITIZEN (MALE): *(Also in a thick, precise, monotonous German accent)* Yes, I too saw ze bucket on his foot. For some reason or other it vas hilarious.

ANDY: So, I searched for the Funny One. I searched all over Europe, Africa, South America, but with no luck—but just that one contact alone lifted my spirits higher, and I started having what I call my Flood o' Fun Notions Phase. Things like...

A DOG NAMED ANTIDISESTABLISHMENTARIANISM

ANDY: *(To the tune of "Bingo Was His Name-O")* There was a farmer had a dog and
    Antidisestablishmentarianism was his name-o *(clap)* -n-t-i-d
    i-s e-s-t
    a-b l-i-s
    h-m e-n-t
    a-r i-a-n
    i-s-m
    Antidisestablishmentarianism was his name-o.
    (clap, clap) t-i-d
    i-s e-s-t
    a-b l-i-s
    h-m
    (He abandons his song and moves along.) Then I started having insights into some of my own foolish behaviour...*(Suddenly turning into the zig-zag fish in the tank:)* Don't try and stop me, Charles, I am going to the other

side of the stage! *(He does.)* Hey, there's another side to the stage! *(He goes in the opposite direction.)*

GERMS WITH HEART CONDITIONS

ANDY: Like when I finish brushing my teeth and I wash off my toothbrush, I wash it under hot water, then, all of a sudden, I switch it over to cold water. *(Mimes quickly switching a toothbrush under the other tap.)* I realized—what I was thinking *way* in the back of my mind—was that *certain germs* that were not killed by the heat of the hot water might die from the shock of going over to the cold water *(mimes frantically switching under cold tap)*—maybe older germs with a heart condition.

SWEET-TALKING MY BOWELS

ANDY: Then I realized, I often talk to different parts of my body—like I often talk to my bowels.
(Looking down towards bowels) Good work there, guys, very good work.

BOWELMAN: *(In indeterminate, passionate, European accent, and looking upwards at* **ANDY***)* Well, you keep the fresh fruit comin' there, Mr. Andy, we'll keep it movin', my friend.

ANDY: *(Looking down)* Gotcha guys...look, guys, I know it isn't easy work...don't think I don't appreciate it...

BOWELMAN: *(Looking up)* Please, Mr. Andy, there's no need to be condescending. We know that we are bowels, eh? You thanked us, that's enough.

We hear the recorded sound of bouzouki music from the movie Zorba the Greek. **ANDY** *does some Greek dancing.*

BOWELMAN: Dance with us. Dance with your bowels!

Greek bouzouki music ends.

ANDY: The incredible Dancing Bowels Scene, here at Weird Andy's Palace of a Thousand Pleasures. Forty-nine years old and still finds bowels funny. And I hear that I'm about to find them funnier in the years to come.

I don't know why, but I always see my bowels as proud, hard-working European immigrants. But their sons and daughters, of course, are doctors and lawyers. And their grandchildren become artists...who revive the bowel dances of their ancestors. (**ANDY** *does some more Greek dancing.*)

ONTARIO GRANDCHILD OF THE BOWELMAN: (*In thick Ontario accent*) Grandpa, please! Teach us the old ways!

BOWELMAN: No, I'm too old...Oh all right! (*He dances again to the Zorba music, speaking as he dances:*) So tell me, children, what do Plato and Aristotle say about the bowels and the dance? Nothing! Hahaha! (*The final song from the movie* Zorba the Greek *plays as he continues to dance; then he bows.*)

ANDY: Just a "notion," just a "fuuuuuun notion." Anybody can have 'em folks—anybody...

Based on this same thought, I came up with this notion of voice-activated prosthetic parts for human bodies...and this also seemed like a Soviet kind of idea to me. So I pictured it taking place in another Soviet think tank where they created an artificial, voice-activated prosthetic leg. Ilya, the last man to have been fitted with the leg, gives me a demonstration.

ILYA'S VOICE-ACTIVATED PROSTHETIC LEG

ILYA: (*A sweet-voiced, innocent, optimistic young Soviet believer*) Yes, I'll demonstrate the leg for you, Mr. Jones. It is a voice-activated leg, you see. Watch! (*He calls clearly to his leg.*)

"Tap three times!" (*His right leg stretches out in front of him, and his extended foot mechanically taps on the floor three distinct times.*)

"Activate ball and pinion!" (*His hips swivel in an unnatural way, causing the prosthetic leg to twist around at an uncomfortable angle.*)

"Bring to a close!" (*His real leg comes up to meet the prosthetic leg. He stands firmly on both legs.*)

"Stiffen!" (*His legs are realigned now, and on the word "Stiffen," he painfully hits himself square on the forehead with the flat of his hand.*)

(*Enthusiastically*) What do you think? Brilliant, of course.

I tell you, Mr. Jones, I was a ballet dancer before my leg was cut off in a threshing machine on a collective farm, but I tell you, my friend, (*fervently:*) I will dance again!

You may be wondering, Mr. Jones, why I hit myself on the forehead at the end of each step cycle: "bring to a close, stiffen" (*hits himself*). It's not simply from self-loathing—although there is some of that of course. (*He laughs*) Hehehehe. No, you see, there's an electronic implant in my forehead and when I hit it, it starts the cycle again. (*He slaps his forehead to demonstrate.*) Oops, now that I've hit the device, I must say all the words again up to the word "stiffen"—it is a Soviet device you see...(*He is forced to say the words again*) "Tap three times, activate ball and pinion, bring to a close, stiffen." Oops, I've done it again, I can't seem to break the habit: "tap three times, activate ball and pinion, bring to a close, stiffen." (*Even though he does not strike his forehead, the leg mysteriously continues; Ilya begins to panic.*) Ooh it's still going! For some reason or other it's still going! Perhaps if I say all the words again..."Tap three times activate ball and pinion bring to a close stiffen, tap three times activate ball and pinion bringtoaclosestiffen." (*All the leg actions repeat, forcing him to walk across the stage.*) IT'S TAKING ME AWAY! "Activate ball and pinion! Activate ball and pinion!" Moscow, we have a problem.

I'll just *sit down*; that will solve the problem! (**ANDY** *sits on the floor, but the leg continues to drag him across the stage; the tapping and the swivelling continue.*) "Activate ball and pinion! Stiffen! Stiffen!" Oh no, the leg's going by itself! (*Prosthetic leg carries him towards the audience:*) "Tap three times activate ball and pinion bring to a close stiffen, tap three times activate ball and pinion bring to a close stiffen!" (*He starts to be pulled through the audience by his leg.*) My God! It's taking me away. Help me, I'm going up the stairs! For God's sake, someone help meeeeee! (**ANDY** *stops and walks back on stage.*)

ANDY: Sad to say, he gyrated out a fourth-storey window, but luckily, he was all right...his leg became detached and went off on its own.

Don't worry, folks. I am going somewhere with all this.

HALF-DOG

ANDY: Then I think (based on my previous thought) that Antidisestablishmentarianism is too long a name for *small* dogs, and you know how they are breeding smaller and smaller dogs...I came up with this idea for "half-dog." I thought of breeding a dog where you just breed the back end out altogether—just front legs. So he just pulls himself along like this. (*Using his index fingers as tiny front legs, he mimes a dog with front legs only, pulling himself forward.*) I've got a picture of it here. (*Reaches into his suitcase, takes out the picture, and shows the audience. It is a very crude, wide-lined drawing of a dog. Where the back legs and the tail would normally be, there is nothing. At that point in the drawing, the dog is bisected by a squiggly line. There is very little effort in this drawing.*)

There it is: half-dog; (*pointing to the dog's back end*) like, he's got no bowels here at the back—it's all gone—no need for bowels—he'd just eat the food, take the nourishment, and then vomit out the dross...

He's very small. And I think "Bingo" is *his* name-o. In fact, you could buy an optional half-dog wheel for $9.95. (*Points to screen, where the image of the dog now has a wheel attached at the back.*)

Just a notion! Just a *fun* notion...I could just jump into the ocean, or I could go to...(*maniacally channelling the fish in the fish tank from the earlier scene*) the other side of the stage! Hahahaha!

(*Goes to the stage right side of the stage, then pivots suddenly on his heel; loses focus, then suddenly notices the other side:*) Hey! There's another side to this stage! (*Goes to stage left side; turns on his heel again for his next idea.*)

FUNERALS FOR ARNOLD SCHWARZENEGGER'S VICTIMS

ANDY: Then I had this notion to hold funerals for every minor character killed in gunfight scenes in American movies, like in that movie *True Lies*, Arnold Schwarzenegger—in that oil barrel scene—throws a hand grenade behind him and like...twenty-five guys are blown up. Nobody cares, they just carry on with the movie. I wanna know who each of those guys was. I wanna have a funeral for every one of those guys, a eulogy, have his wife and kids there.

> *There is tinny organ funeral music as he walks as if to a funeral chapel podium.*

FUNERAL EMCEE: We are here today to celebrate the life of Naldred Ameshi, the...ah...fictional character who was killed in that oil barrel scene in *True Lies*. (*Nods to Naldred's wife:*) Mrs. Ameshi.

MRS. AMESHI: (*She speaks very softly, with an unspecific accent.*) Naldred was a father, a son, a husband, and a brother. I feel it was someone else speaking when he said...

MOVIE BAD GUY: (*He speaks harshly and bitterly, in movie bad-guy accent:*) Well, I guess world domination will not be ours this time. But at least we are still alive. We will kill again!

MRS. AMESHI: This was not the man we knew...Perhaps it was the American scriptwriter talking. You know...many of the other men killed in that scene were also from our village...how many more thousands of lives were filled with grief just from the oil barrel scene alone, how many childhoods lived, years of nurturing, only to be sent to America to have the issues simplified and then to be killed by Arnold Schwarzenegger.

BOILING OIL ON ROBIN HOOD'S NOT-SO-MERRY MEN

ANDY: I'd even deal with the characters who fall off battlements in Robin Hood movies. Like this...

NEWFOUNDLAND WOMAN: *(Speaking with a quiet and gentle West Country Newfoundland accent)* Yes, yes come in, come in, Mr. Jones, 'e's in 'ere. *(She points.)* He had boiling oil poured on ees legs the last time Robin 'ood attacked the castle. *(She beckons, and they walk into the young man's room. She gestures towards a young man in bed.)* "Rob from the rich, give to de poor" is all very well, Mr. Jones, but look at the boiling-oil damage to ees legs." *(Mimes pulling back the man's blanket.)*

ANDY: *(Recoiling)* Good God!

> She puts back the blanket and beckons **ANDY**; they walk out of the young man's room.

NEWFOUNDLAND WOMAN: Yes, Mr. Jones...'e can't work in the fields now; 'e can't be a soldier; what can 'e do?...

DAMAGED SOLDIER: *(As if from the next room)* I'm not *useless*, Mother!

NEWFOUNDLAND WOMAN: Of course not, dear. Mother was only joking. I'll be in to sing you a song. Run along, Mr. Jones...*(She shoos Jones out, turns her back on the audience as she goes back in the soldier's room. She sings to the tune of "I'm a Little Dutch Girl.")*
I'll sing a song o' soldiers and pretty girls and dances,
I'll sing a song o' soldiers and glory and *(pause—she turns to where* **ANDY** *would presumably be and whispers)* Death! *(Then* **ANDY** *continues quietly to sing the soldier's mother's song:)*
I'll sing a song of soldiers and pretty girls and dances.
(Turns back to the audience.) I'll sing a song of soldiers and glory and *(pause)* Death!

ANDY: I don't know, maybe I'm naive. Maybe I'm always just headin' in the wrong direction...

Once again channelling the fish in the tank, he suddenly sees the other side of the stage, walks across, walks back. Then, out of nowhere, he does a quick bit.

IRISH LAMENT

ANDY: *(desperate Irishman:)* An Irishman's lament: Why am I depressed? Why am I depressed? A: it's Christmas; B: I'm in Killarney; and C: all the effin' folks are at home.

The first few bars of the song "Christmas in Killarney" play. This music morphs into the "Telstar" theme, and the eerie special lighting transforms the stage back into the Whizgiggian dimension. JORELLO *is beamed in and stands in his usual centre spotlight in the middle of the Mayan circle.*

CRUCIAL CHEESEBURGER, PART FIVE:
THE COMEDIANS' ENTRANCE

JORELLO: *(Still in his formal educational style)* Our only hope of breaking through might lie in the very *foolishness* of the idea. He might just cotton on to it and realize who he is—because for the humans, the more improbable, the more they love the notion. The great unprovables have always been their favourite beliefs, the ones they die for; the existence of God comes to mind, but my favourite? Life after death.

Have you ever seen a human corpse? Three days out in the warm and that person's body is rotten filth, stink, and disease. In what possible sense will the living ever laugh and share an anecdote with these decaying creatures again? It is such a ludicrous idea. Surely someone hanging around the comedians' entrance came up with that one! And if the humans so easily believe it—then why can't An-dee believe that we exist? If he would believe it, we could swoop in and save him. He would be erased from human memory. He would never have existed in the human sphere. But time is running out. And we must face the fact that the crucial foodstuff is in his suitcase at this very moment. It is number 1,347 of a foodstuff called...*(His lips find it hard to say this foreign word)* "cheeseburger"—and if even one molecule of that food passes his lips, it would render him a hopeless candidate for reintegration into the purity of our dimension—and furthermore, the gas-producing nature of that food would cause spontaneous combustion during the enormous pressure of re-entry.

> *There is a very quick lighting change, bringing us back to the human dimension. There is a recording of canned laughter—***ANDY*** has apparently just said something very funny during* **JORELLO***'s previous speech.*

THE ONE-MAN SQUARE DANCE

ANDY: You laugh. *(The canned laughter happens again;* **ANDY** *laughs.)* You laugh—*(milder canned laughter)* but I think I *am* part of the modern dance. And of course, I'm concerned about the modern dance—every day I think about it—but the thing that really worries me is the traditional dance. Sometimes I think I might be the only one left who cares! A day might come when I'd be forced to dance the square set by myself...

Ladies and gentlemen, the "One-Man Lancers"!

> *The traditional fiddle tune "Mussels in the Corner" starts fast and gradually speeds up as* **ANDY** *frantically dances a one-man version of a Newfoundland square dance called "The Lancers." He desperately tries to do the moves of all eight dancers. This piece is about the fear, the thrill, the panic of being in a fast-moving square dance with a bunch of crazed dancers. The moves below are an approximate version of The Lancers:*
>
> *First position—upstage centre.*
> *With arms in the air, he step-dances in place.*

With one arm raised, he holds the hand of his imaginary partner and walks fast to downstage front, dipping under the imaginary arms of the opposite couple.

He gives a look of mild panic to the audience for a second, then goes backwards under the same imaginary arms.

Walks backwards to his first position.

Immediately upon landing in first position, he is pulled by an incredible imaginary force into the hand-over-hand movements all the way to stage right—in fact, out of the centre light into the outer reaches of stage right.

Then he is frantically pulled hand over hand across the stage to the outer reaches of stage left.

Pivoting wildly, he is then pulled hand over hand across stage to stage right—but still staying in the centre area.

While dancing in place, he removes his outer shirt frantically. He is obviously overheated.

In Michael Flatley Irish-dancing style, he glides across to stage left— also still in the centre area—and step-dances in place for a few worried seconds.

Dances right and with his right hand holds the right hand of an imaginary man for the intense "men step out" moment, wherein two men, face to face, step-dance wildly and competitively while holding each other's right hands.

He is then pulled out of "men step out" to a standard "swing your partner" swing by an imaginary large, powerful partner.

There are two giddy swings with the imaginary large partner; they disengage, he bows to that large partner.

With growing terror, he observes the "thread the needle" action taking place in front of him on stage right. Registering his fear, he makes a sign of the cross and dives into "thread the needle."

"Thread the needle" is carried out as follows: his fisted right arm shoots in the air as the crook of his left arm wipes the top of his head, as if he is going under the other couple's joined arms. Then, quickly, his fisted left arm shoots in the air as the crook of his right arm wipes the top *of his head, as if he is going under the next couple's joined arms. Repeats these "thread the needle" moves several times.*

Returns, reeling drunkenly, to centre stage.

Repeats the opening walk downstage and the backwards walk back. Suddenly swivels while back-to-back with his imaginary partner in a circle ["couples out around"]. He collapses onto his back—prone—in centre, with feet directly towards the audience.

On the floor from a prone position, he continues step-dancing in the air. The audience sees the bottom of his feet.

While he's on his back, his next steps are fancy "on the floor" break-dancing steps. He includes some sideways can-can kicks. Then he turns and, lying on his side, does a full body rotation on the floor, starting by crawling upwards towards stage right, keeping his hip/buttock off the floor. He ends up with his feet pointed at the audience.

He finishes the dance with a complete death-collapse, legs spread and arms at his side on the floor.

Ideally, his face is in the middle of the circle.

FUNNIEST HUMAN IN THE WORLD ARRIVES

ANDY: Ladies and gentlemen, remember earlier in the evening, I told you that this evening would lead to a special moment—that our purpose would become crystal clear.

There might even be an insight!

I think this might be the moment...I don't want to put too much pressure on myself. But I was thinking I might try the Funniest Human Being in the World myself...What do you think? (*He elicits a response from the audience; they applaud—hopefully. He goes over to suitcase, gasps, drinks water.*) I am no chicken of the spring, my friend.

I got all the Funniest One's stuff here in my suitcase. Now what did the German woman say? She said (*imitating her German accent*), "Half of him vas painted blue; ze other half vas white."

(*He starts putting blue makeup on the right side of his face, head, and ear, and white makeup on the left side of his face, head, and ear.*) Of course, blue and white. Utter simplicity, yet more complex than simply black and white—yeeeeeeees, *most* fertile ground for comedy. (*He finishes covering his face and ears with blue and white makeup. There is a sharp vertical demarcation down the middle of his forehead, nose, top lip, and neck. He is divided in half—right down the middle.*)

"In place of his own nose, he vas wearing a pig's nose." (*He puts an elastic around his head. It has a pig's nose attached.*) Of course, that's pretty obvious—the pig being the sacrificial beast of comic ritual. Live like pigs/all men are pigs/the shitting pig/your room is like a pigsty—all those famous phrases.

"He vas vearing one half of a small, white, fluffy Hitler-style moustache, but white and fluffy you know." Ah, yes, of course! Hitler's moustache! (*He picks half of a white moustache out of the suitcase.*) The most frightening piece of body hair in the history of Western civilization—but in this case (*meaningfully*) just half of it, and that "white and fluffy"...ah yes, makes perfect sense. (*Attaches the white half-moustache.*)

"For a hat he vas vearing a shell." (*Picks up the soft white "shell" hat. He thinks hard about this one—then it dawns on him.*) Oh! I see, the perfectly *unfunny* hat—which creates a vacuum into which is sucked our collective memory of all *funny* hats throughout history...brilliant!

"His foot vas stuck in a bucket." (*Puts his foot firmly into a white plastic beef bucket—his foot is stuck.*) Plato says that the Foot in the Bucket is the crossroads of comedy and tragedy—laughter and tears coming together. (*He does a repeating laughter-to-tears comedy bit. It is a lazzi loop of guffawing/weeping, laughing/sobbing:*) Hahahaha...whoo whoo whoo whoo. And! Of course, Oedipus Rex actually means "King with the bucket on his foot"—approximately. (*Then he puts the metal crown on his head—over the shell hat.*)

Now, ladies and gentlemen, I am merely the conduit for this sacred moment, so I must ensure that I myself do not derive any pleasure from any laughter that might ensue, and I'll do that with this special comedy device of incredible pain which I have right here...

> **ANDY** *places his arm in a splint-like device. It is made of two forearm-length sticks held together by two thin leather belts. He buckles the belts to secure the device to his forearm. There are large, sharp bolts*

which have been screwed into the sides of the sticks and consequently into his arm. Then, with a ratchet, he appears to drive these bolts further into the flesh of his forearm. He dramatically tightens them, appearing to cause excruciating pain, while struggling to keep up a dramatically brave face. He continues to explain his balderdash.

ANDY: ...thus rendering myself a "vestal virgin of the ludicrous," retroactively of course. *(He continues to ratchet the screws.)* My gaining any pleasure from this event would be the equivalent of dirt in the test tube of this experiment. *(He is bravely ratcheting the bolt even tighter and over-indicating that his pain is nearly unbearable. Then he becomes the German tourist again:)* "He vas saying something frightening, then he vas making a loud noise like AAAArrgghhhhh!"

Okay, here goes. *(He makes four clumping bucket steps across the stage. He stops. He raises his fists to the heavens and shouts a guttural noise, as if he is angry at God:)* AAAArrgghhhhh! *(He turns abruptly to the audience to see if it worked— it didn't; no one is laughing.)* No, it's not working. I'll try again. *(He makes four more bucket steps across the stage in the opposite direction; stops; shouts the noise again:)* AAAArrgghhhhh! *(Looks at audience again—not working.)* No, no. Maybe if I try some of my own comedy material with it. *(He re-enacts* "Ilya's Prosthetic Leg":) Tap three times. *(He taps his bucket-foot three times.)* Activate ball and pinion; bring to a close; stiffen! AAAArrgghhhhh! *(He pivots, walks in the opposite direction then re-enacts the "Oil on Her Breasts" guy:)* When the ball and pinion was activated, it squirted oil all over their breasts. AAAArrgghhhhh! *(He pivots again.)* The dance of the bowels! *(He does the Greek dancing while making his own bouzouki-like noises:)* Da da dada dad da dadadada.

No. It's not working—sorry, sorry, this is the most *unfunny* moment in my career. Plato's absolute "Actor's Nightmare"—funny costume, no funny lines...What am I doing this for? I shouldn't have tried this, obviously...it's too dangerous.

Crestfallen and defeated, **ANDY** *trudges back to the suitcase to take off all his stuff. Then he suddenly stops and realizes something. He then* *turns around slowly, almost menacingly, to face the audience with an otherworldly, ecstatic gleam in his eye. A moment of revelation? Or of utter madness.*

ANDY: Wait! Wait…of course! Of course! Now I see! Now I see! Whizgiggan is real! I *am* An-dee. That would explain why I always feel like a pretend human being—like when I go to the hockey rink with the kids, I think, "Wow, I'm getting to hang out with the human beings—I hope they don't find out I'm not one of them."

Of course! How else could the Whizgiggians get through to me except through this utterly ludicrous fictional moment. Yes, now today when poor old God is dead—and Jean Paul Sartre rules the roost—yes, the simple truth had to come in the back door—through the comedians' entrance. Good Lord! *(Happily, confidentially:)* Now I see!

CALLING ON GOD/GIVING UP ON GOD

ANDY: In fact, ladies and gentlemen, if God is *not* dead, perhaps he too could use this little opening in the dimensions *(mimes opening curtains)* to make himself known to us. *("Begging the heavens" gesture:)* Come on! Pleeeeeeease! Come on! Give us a sign! *(Having a joyous thought:)* God on stage at the LSPU Hall—the ultimate leap o' faith. *(Quietly:)* Please. *(Beat.)* *(Deeply disappointed, and through his sobs, he cries out again with a more resigned disgust at God:)* Arrrrrrgh.

(Then, to the audience, quietly) Goodbye, everyone.

I'm going back to Whizgiggan, where I belong—back to the place that knows not death, that needs not God. Goodbye.

CRUCIAL CHEESEBURGER, PART SIX:
THEY ARE COMING TO GET ME

*Music and lighting changes bring us back to the Whizgiggian dimension. In a pre-recorded scene, we see **JORELLO** on a screen. He is in an extreme fish-eye lens close-up. He is on location in a helicopter, where* *he wears a Second World War bomber jacket and earphones. He is extremely excited. This is a turning point in Whizgiggian history. This is their "Jesus rising from the dead" moment.*

JORELLO: *(On the screen)* Whizgiggians! Did you hear that? We've broken through! He now knows we are real. He wants to come home—we have finally broken through, and he hasn't eaten the Crucial Cheeseburger. It's still in his suitcase; we're goin' in!!! An-dee, we are coming to get you!

There is an Apocalypse Now helicopter sound montage as they swoop in to rescue him. The two dimensions have come together now. There are elements of Whizgiggian and human lighting and sound mixed.)

ANDY: *(Taking the cheeseburger out of the suitcase slowly.)* They're comin' to get me, goodbye! You'll forget I ever lived. I'll be annihilated from the memory of the human past; my parents will never have had me; I will not have loved, then had to lose my loved ones. I *can* choose...I can choose not to have been born!!!!! *(Bringing the Crucial Cheeseburger near his mouth, he thinks about it, then to audience:)*
Or...
I could bite the Crucial Cheeseburger. What should I do? Bite the cheeseburger or be assumed into Whizgiggan? What should I do? Tell me. *(He asks the audience. He ad libs...cheeseburger? Whizgiggan? He listens to their advice, then he absentmindedly, accidentally eats the cheeseburger. He is shocked by what he has done; a silly "oh noooooo" look comes across his face. The choice has been made—albeit accidentally. It is too late—he is irreversibly a human now. Helicopter sounds and Whizgiggian lighting fade away forever.)*
Oh no. Oh no. Whenever I get stressed like that, I always eat something. *(Looking up:)* And now they're gone. And I never got to choose! *(He sobs piteously as he continues to eat the cheeseburger—chomping and sobbing mixed together. He starts to exit, still whimpering, his bucketed foot loudly clomping on the floor.)*

KING O' FUN: FINAL REPORT TO THE WORLD

Stops, seeing the audience as if for the first time; all Whizgiggian reality has faded from his memory. He speaks in a thick West Country Newfoundland accent.

ANDY: Hmmm, what does't ye people 'ere. Oh yes! You'm the King o' Fun People. How long have ye been 'ere.

STRANGE AUDIENCE MEMBER: *(Disgusted)* Hours!

ANDY: *(Dropping out of character)* Hours? It's only been an hour and twenty minutes—but I know what you mean. *(He gets back into his West Country Newfoundland character.)* You'm here for the King o' Fun Report... I'm sorry. Well, I guess this were my report. I get to give up the crown now. Been a year and a day. That was the bargain. It were a good year, but it were enough. I'm glad that it's over.

ANDY hands the metal crown to a random audience member.

ANDY: *(To the audience member:)* You'm takin over now. Good luck. *(Aside:)* Long live the King! (or Queen)...*(Then he heads back to centre stage with the bucket still on his foot and, suddenly remembering something, he speaks in a German accent.)*

GERMAN MAN: Now I remember ze Funniest One in ze World, he vas *saying* something...he vas saying, "I think I vill go to ze other side of ze room." *(Laughing all the while and like the fish in the tank, he clumsily crosses the stage with the bucket still on his foot. He pivots suddenly and goes in the opposite direction.)*
"I think I vill go to ze other side of ze room." *(He stops. Still laughing and channelling the dim, innocent fish in the tank, he re-crosses with the bucket still on his foot.)* Or maybe it vas *(degenerating into a German-accented gibberish:)* "I thimke I wikkle go to ze uzzer sidle of ze room-boom."

(He finds that very, very funny.) Hahaha!

Or something very hilarious like that. Or maybe...

"I thikjm iujhgbjk goo toool utto shede lokmomb gwui wis geee wiz-zzygeeee gggeeee."

> **ANDY**'s *words become less and less intelligible until he holds his hand over his own mouth, desperately trying to stifle the explosive whizgig-ging-style laughter that erupts from his very soul. He disappears into the Whizgiggian dimension.*

> *Blackout.*

King o' Fun was first presented at the LSPU Hall, St. John's, Newfoundland and Labrador, on May 2, 1997. The show was produced by the Resource Centre for the Arts Theatre Company.

Performed by **ANDY JONES** with **MARY-LYNN BERNARD** as Darlene

Direction and dramaturgy by **CHARLIE TOMLINSON**

Script written by **ANDY JONES**

Concept by **ANDY JONES** and **CHARLIE TOMLINSON**

Stage manager/Sound operator: **KELLY JONES**

Lighting design by **FLIP JANES**

Sound compilation by **DON ELLIS**

Music: "Telstar" by the Tornados (1962); Lancers' music **BERNARD FELIX**; Andean music by **ANYI**

Set design by **SHELLEY CORNICK** and **PAUL WADE**

Comedy Device of Incredible Pain design and construction by **PAUL WADE**

Rooster Bishop of Borino design and construction **JANE TOMLINSON**
Movement coach: **ANNE TROAKE**
Publicity: **BRENDA O'BRIEN**
Poster: **GEOFF YOUNGHUSBAND**
Photography: **JUSTIN HALL**
Stage technician: **GEOFF YOUNGHUSBAND**
Production assistant: **MARY-LYNN BERNARD**
Company administration: **NICOLE ROUSSEAU**

And special thanks to the LSPU Hall Staff, the Newfoundland and Labrador Arts Council, the City of St. John's Arts Jury, and the Government of Newfoundland and Labrador's Tourism, Culture and Recreation Department.

TOURING HISTORY

From May 2 to 11, 1997, the first version of *King o' Fun* played in St. John's, Newfoundland, at the LSPU Hall. It was produced by the Resource Centre for the Arts Theatre Company under Artistic Animateur Lois Brown.

King o' Fun was part of Eastern Front's 1997–98 theatre season in Halifax, Nova Scotia. That performance was directed by Jillian Keiley.

In 2004–2005 Andy Jones embarked on a national tour of *King o' Fun* that included the Nakai Theatre, Whitehorse, Yukon; the Klondike Institute of Art & Culture, Dawson City, Yukon; One Yellow Rabbit's High Performance Rodeo, Calgary, Alberta; Intrepid Theatre, Victoria, British Columbia; George Ryga Centre, Penticton, British Columbia; the Firehall Theatre, Vancouver, British Columbia; Western Canada Theatre Company, Kamloops, British Columbia; Workshop West Playwrights' Theatre's KaBoom! Festival, Edmonton, Alberta; Eastern Front Theatre's On the Waterfront Festival, Halifax, Nova Scotia; Magnetic North Theatre Festival, Ottawa, Ontario; Seabird Theatre Festival, Newtown, Newfoundland and Labrador; Rising Tide Theatre,

Trinity, Newfoundland and Labrador; Gros Morne Theatre Festival, Cow Head, Newfoundland and Labrador; Beaches Heritage Centre, Eastport, Newfoundland and Labrador; and the Live Bait Theatre Festival in Sackville, New Brunswick.

In September of 2006, a filmed version of *King o' Fun* was aired on Bravo and screened at the Atlantic Film Festival in Halifax. This film was directed for TV by Mike Jones.

PRODUCTION NOTES

There were many versions of this show between 1997 and 2006. The version herein is based on the May 3, 1997, and the December 18, 2004, performances at the LSPU Hall.

As in all of Andy Jones's shows, the order of scenes was often changed, and the sketches, bits, and monologues came and went during the life of *King o' Fun*. Some of the sketches were from the CODCO TV and stage shows, others were newly minted, and some were recycled from Andy Jones's previous shows. The Whizgiggian content, however, stayed consistent throughout these variations.

This show was originally done without any video effects. These effects can be quite easily removed from a production of this show. The floor cloth is also optional.

Props, Costumes, and Set Pieces

Darlene's bridal costumes: wedding dress with skirt hanging in front only, wedding dress train attached to back of dress but able to be pulled away and held in the crook of the bride's arm, bride's veil, white stockings, garter belt, lacy white underwear, white wedding shoes, and bouquet.

Andy's basic costume: black T-shirt, grey shirt, dark trousers, belt (de-looped at top of show), black shoes, black socks, black underwear shorts, a wristwatch, a pair of glasses in pocket.

Costumes and makeup which are to be pre-set as props: a soft, realistic, cloth crown, as well as metal *King o' Fun* crowns—one is to be given away each night; Aristotle's laurel crown; a bishop's mitre; a rubber pig's nose with elastic strap; one half of a white, fluffy, Hitler-style moustache; double-sided tape for moustache; a shell hat; a plastic beef bucket; a container of blue makeup; and a container of white makeup.

Props and set pieces: There is a twenty-foot by twenty-foot canvas floor cloth. Painted on this floor cloth is a large circle; inside the circle is a Mayan-style image of a man suppressing a laugh by holding his hand over his mouth. Around the edges of the circle, there are symbols such as the individual elements of the basic formula: H^∞ x F (1,911) = F^1, as well as symbols representing topics from the show, such as a cheeseburger, bishop's mitre, crown, fish, laurel crown, oil can, DNA symbol, prosthetic leg, half-dog, etc. There is a movie-style screen on the upstage wall, one black wooden chair, and on stage left, a hard suitcase opened toward the audience. Inside or behind this suitcase, there are the following items: an edible cheeseburger in a small fast-food takeout container; a large, realistic but artificial rose; the rubber pig's nose; the comedy device of incredible pain; a ratchet-style wrench; the rooster bishop hand puppet; a rough drawing of "half-dog"; a copy of the *Dictionary of Newfoundland English*; a bottle of water; and a towel.

There are also three eleven- by seventeen-inch cardboard panels with crude drawings showing the three stages of overacting.

AN EVENING WITH UNCLE VAL

by Andy Jones

with Michael Jones Sr.

TABLE OF CONTENTS

A catalogue of the recitations and monologues of Uncle Val, as well as the ensuing one-man sketches, commentaries, and reminiscences of Andy Jones contained in *An Evening with Uncle Val*.

Part One

St. John's—A Bayman's Perspective, by Uncle Val 125
Uncle Val: The Origin Story 127
When the Wrestling Seemed Real, by Uncle Val 129
Vince Meets the Beatles, by Uncle Val 131
Joey Smallwood on My Mind 134
I Take the Bullet for JFK 135
Gold Medal at the Seniors' Olympics, by Uncle Val 137
"Ode to Tea," by Uncle Val 140
Shakespeare in the Burbs, by Uncle Val 141

Parliament of Cultural Romance...143
Parliament of Cultural Romance: Townie Imposter.........................146
Mauled at the Teddy Bears' Picnic, by Uncle Val.........................148
Meet My Mentor, Francis Colbert...150

Part Two

Love in the Time of Colic, by Uncle Val.................................154
Cubist Theatre..156
I Take the Bullet for JFK, Part Two: Bob Marley & Jackie O..............157
Death—Real and Imagined, by Uncle Val...................................158
75 Candles: Val's Birthday, by Uncle Val................................160
Tool Time for Danes...163
There's a Tavern in Distress, by Uncle Val..............................164
Parliament of Cultural Romance: The Politics of Fish....................165
Farewell to Cozy Cul-de-Sacs by Uncle Val...............................168

ANDY JONES'S NOTES ON *AN EVENING WITH UNCLE VAL*

I wrote the first letter from Uncle Val shortly after I met Francis Colbert from Job's Cove, Conception Bay.

I first saw Francis perform his recitations at the Good Entertainment Festival at Killdevil Camp on Newfoundland's west coast in 1978. I loved his performances so much that I started imitating him, and I soon started to write dialogue for a new character based on my best impersonation of Francis. The character was called Val Reardigan—or Uncle Val, as he would be respectfully addressed in his own community.

Uncle Val was, like Francis himself, an outharbour Newfoundlander and a former fisherman. Since I was a suburban townie and knew almost nothing of outharbour life, I made Val an unwilling prisoner in suburban St. John's—forced to live there with his daughter, his son-in-law, their two children, and their poodles.

My father, Michael Jones Sr., provided me with Val's "senior citizen" medical and emotional details. I lifted lots of phrases and insights directly from my conversations with my very witty and kind-hearted dad.

Val's observations are in the form of letters to his friend Jack, and they chronicle family life in "back of town" St. John's—where I myself grew up.

In 1978 Bill Squires from CBC St. John's put Val's first letter on the air and encouraged me to write more. Eventually I wrote over thirty pieces.

In 2006, with the help of director Lois Brown, I decided to put a bunch of them together and attempt to give some context about the world in which they had been written.

The letters were originally created during those heady days that were referred to as the "cultural renaissance" of Newfoundland and Labrador. I therefore made a valiant attempt in *An Evening with Uncle Val* to explain the feelings of an innocent, enthusiastic bunch of young artists who were the first generation of Newfoundland and Labrador *Canadians*.

And of course—as I always do in my one-man shows—I also threw in a few unrelated sketches and bits. I justify this by calling it "Cubist Theatre."

If there are any young ones out there who would like to make Uncle Val live again, please be my guest.

—AJ, December 2023

PART ONE

The time: 1986–1990

The setting: A suburban basement apartment in St. John's, Newfoundland and Labrador.

A high pyramid of different-sized cardboard boxes is piled along the upstage wall. At centre stage, just in front of this cardboard pyramid, there is a lower stack of boxes.

Someone is obviously in the process of moving.

Stretching across the stage, in front of the cardboard boxes, are a few simple furnishings suggesting several locations in this basement apartment. At extreme stage right, there is a coat tree with a winter coat, a scarf, and a salt-and-pepper cap hanging on it. Next to the coat tree there is a small wooden writing table with a chair, a pen, some writing paper, envelopes, and stamps. There is a lamp on the writing table, which has an area rug underneath it.

At centre stage, just in front of the lower stack of boxes, there is a reinforced box that provides an ideal seat for moments of reflection or a soapbox for stand-up ranting. This is the "soapbox/throne."

Slightly stage left of centre, there is a large wooden doll's house. The doll's house rests on a toy box.

Just downstage from the doll's house, there is a large outdoor metal garbage can with a cover.

Stage left of the doll's house, the kitchen area is suggested by a chrome table and two chrome chairs. On the table are tea-making implements, including an electric kettle, cups, a box of Tetley tea, a can of Carnation milk, a sugar bowl, a box of Purity Lemon Creams Biscuits, and a few plates.

Farther stage left of the kitchen area (and outside the apartment) there is a Canada Post letter box.

As the lights begin to dim, the pre-show music cross-fades into a recording of the "Portuguese Waltzes" played on the guitar by Duane Andrews.
The lights come up on **UNCLE VAL**, *a young seventy-something outharbour Newfoundlander, seated at his writing table. He quietly writes for a few seconds before he speaks aloud the words he is writing. He has a soft, melodious Job's Cove accent.*

ST. JOHN'S—A BAYMAN'S PERSPECTIVE, BY UNCLE VAL

VAL: December 1, 1986

Dear Jack, *(With his head down, he writes as he speaks.)* Thank you for your letter of the thirteenth. *(He then looks up and faces the audience directly—they have become Jack.)* Well, as you know, I'm still here in St. John's. Sometimes I feel like writing to you and saying, "Help! I am a prisoner in St. John's!" But I know you'd think: There goes that melodramatic old fool again. But I'm quite serious. People in St. John's are very strange. They keep saying things like *(heroically:)* "There's nothing like a cup of tea in the woods."

I mean, they say that quite often.

I keep picturing a cup of tea all by itself in the woods. And I agree there would be nothing quite like that.

I'm living here with my daughter Margaret. She married a man from St. John's. I tried to stop her from marrying Bernard, but I could not at that time present a coherent case. It was more instinctual.

I instinctually hated Bernard.

Bernard is in Insurance. Insurance is in Bernard...*(mumbling to himself:)* In fact, I believe Insurance is *up* Bernard. **(VAL** *stands up on left side of his writing table.)* My only comfort these days is a friend of mine across the road. He's from Bonavista Bay.

Occasionally we get together and cry our way through the *Fisherman's Broadcast*...Bernard thinks the *Fisherman's Broadcast* is beamed in from another planet.

And their youngsters. Oh my, oh my. Jimmy and Kimmy. Rhyming youngsters.

Children are funny in St. John's. Here they learn by *asking questions...* Now in my day, Jack, you did not ask questions—I mean, you had questions inside you, but you had to sit around the kitchen until someone accidentally expelled an answer which you then joined to a question, jigsaw-style. Sometimes in the old days, there'd be three or four youngsters sitting on the daybed and someone would let fly with a piece of information—you could almost hear the wheels turning *(he mimes wheels turning by the side of his head)*, and their little eyes would glow with enlightenment. *(VAL imitates the voice of a child at a crucial moment of realization:)* So, they'd think, *that's how Elizabeth come to be livin' at the Pottles'!*

Often that was how Elizabeth herself found out.

And in those days, children ran messages. That was their job. And in return they were allowed to sleep indoors.

But nowadays it's all Spider-Man and *Dukes of Hazzard* and Chef Boyardee Scarios. I'd give 'em a scario. I'd like to run into their bedroom on Christmas morning and say, "Jimmy, Kimmy, wake up! Spider-Man is dead! Yes, they finally got 'en. He's lying out now in some cheap, second-rate funeral home, just like you will be someday. Your little white bodies laid out in little white coffins—and the skin that was once your face will slither off your skull and be eaten by worms!!!"

Then they'd take notice of their grandfather. *(Returns to sit in his chair.)*

But of course, I never say nothin'. Not in St. John's.

(Once again, he writes with his pen as he looks down at the paper, speaking as he writes.)

Trusting that you and Madonna are well, I remain,

Your friend,

Valentine

P.S.: They also got two dogs, poodles—Tiffy and Tuffy...oh, and I presume everyone out home knows by now that Margaret is expecting. Her third. Oh my. *(He sighs.)*

> He walks to downstage centre and, dropping the **UNCLE VAL** character, does an informal introduction to the show.

UNCLE VAL: THE ORIGIN STORY

ANDY: Good evening, ladies, and gentlemen. Welcome to *An Evening with Uncle Val*. My name is Andy Jones. Uncle Val is a character that I've been performing since 1978. He's an outharbour Newfoundlander in his seventies, a retired fisherman, who through circumstances beyond his control has ended up living in St. John's. He comes into St. John's for a series of eye operations and then ends up living with daughter Margaret and son-in-law Bernard—much against his will at the beginning.

The recitations are all in the form of letters to his friend Jack at home, and they are in fact almost entirely about St. John's, or more exactly about middle-class, suburban St. John's reality—since those are my own personal roots. In fact, all those years I was writing Uncle Val, I pictured him living in a particular house on Shea Street which was part of my old paper route when I was a kid...in fact, this house right here! As luck would have it...(**ANDY** *indicates the doll's house—surprised that it is there. It is a model of the house that* **VAL** *lives in.*)

But it's all seen through the eyes of Val—the outsider.

For the purposes of this evening, I'm assuming you don't know anything at all about Val. I'll be explaining it all to you almost as if you were a Danish audience. This is something I often do. I prepare my shows for Denmark and thus assume you don't even know where Newfoundland *is*. So if I seem overly explanatory it's because I'm trying to get through those thick Danish heads. (*He knocks on his own head, walks back to desk, has a new thought, returns to front lit area.*) I figure I'm on pretty safe ground doing anti-Danish material. I mean who's gonna say anything. Probably no Danes in the audience here tonight. (*Uh-oh, he sees some Danes.*) Uh-oh, there is.

Sorry, there's a Danish couple up there in the back row. Sorry, sorry sir, there are no live sex acts in the show tonight. (*Sympathetically:*) Sorry. (*Then rolls his eyes:*) Oh, the Danes! That's all they want to see. Apparently, they do Ibsen in the nude in Copenhagen. (*Heads back to chair, stops, has a new thought, returns to front lit area.*)

If you have ever lived in downtown St. John's and you're not Danish, you've probably heard that opening letter thirty or forty times. It's interesting—that part about the "little white bodies in little white coffins"—I wrote that waaaay before I had kids. After I had kids, I felt really bad about it…But I haven't been able to come up with anything better, so I left it there. So if you have any ideas, let me know after the show. 'Course when you start off as a young comedian like that, you want to come up with the most shocking material. When I first started out, I used to do this piece called "The Soft-Spot Murderer." You know that soft spot that babies have on their heads? (*He feels the spot on his own head.*) Picture the scene. It's the nursery in your local hospital, and up comes the "Soft-Spot Murderer." (*With his killer index finger ready, he does exaggerated sneaking-up movements as he makes mystery music climax sounds.*) Dant dant dant dant daaaa da da da da (*a quick breath, then, he mimes his index finger poking down, deep into a soft spot:*) sploosh! (*He repeats the whole sequence*). Dant dant dant dant daaaa da da da da sploosh!

After I had kids, I felt really bad about that. 'Course after they became teenagers, I didn't feel so bad…

Anyway, here's Val. He's in St John's. He's not happy. He's even cold towards his own grandchildren. He's a bit of a misery, really. At this point he's ready to go home again. (*He pauses, then he over-explains what he is doing on the stage.*)

And now I'm going to go over there. (*He walks behind the writing table.*) I *was* over there (*points to where he was*) and now I'm here. And that's just for variety. Earlier, you remember, I walked all the way over there. (*He goes to centre in front of centre soapbox/throne, then points to extreme stage left.*) You saw me over there. (*Then, pointing to extreme upstage left:*) Later on I'll walk behind that table at some point (*pointing to the chrome kitchen table*)…and later on I'll actually go all the way around here (*walks behind boxes from stage right to stage left*). I will disappear from view for a second. (*He disappears for a second.*) (*He stops; split-second pause; dramatic re-entry.*) And re-emerge right here! (*He is now out in front of the soapbox/throne.*) You are kinda like fish in a fish tank; you'll think "Wow, this is pretty exciting."

People will say to you, "You saw Andy Jones's show. What did you think?" You'll say, "Well, b'y, he was all over the stage. That's worth fifteen bucks right there." *(He walks to writing desk and sits.)*

WHEN THE WRESTLING SEEMED REAL, BY UNCLE VAL

VAL: January 6, 1987, Old Christmas Day

Dear Jack, Thanks to you and Madonna for the card and the enclosed snaps. *(He sighs.)*

Looks like it was a wonderful Christmas party. *(Looks up at audience, which has become Jack.)* I'm glad I missed it, in a way. I'd-a probably only got drunk...and sang...and danced. *(Big sigh.)*

Well, nothing much to report here from the Capital, except Bernard and Margaret got "the cable," which means we get to watch *Golden Girls* three times in the same night. And now Bernard makes us watch a lot of *bowling* on channel nine. I always reckon you'd want to be fairly desperate to even *go* bowling, let alone watch someone else doing it, but it excites Bernard, and he is master of the remote control.

In the morning, Jimmy and Kimmy are in charge, so I spend my time with *Mr. Dressup* and *The Friendly Giant*. This morning, Mr. Dressup had on pictures of a vegetable orchestra. There was a cucumber playing a fiddle, a pea on trumpet, and a watermelon dancing.

This is preparing children for the harsh realities of life.

Poor Bernard was at the office and missed it.

Now I remember when there was only one channel and even the wrestling seemed real. Oh, that was the golden age of TV, back then. Remember the wrestling, Jack? Oh my, you took your life in your hands if you so much as *spoke* during the wrestling. I knew three people in our community alone who choked to death on their food from the excitement of watching the wrestling. Remember Hard Boiled Haggerty, Jack? And Gorgeous George and Gene Kiniski—remember him? He was a mean fella. And there was Lord Athol Layton. And the midgets. And Bobo Brazil with his Coco Bonk, Haystack Calhoun, Little Beaver, Sky Low Low and them. I remember there was an old fella out home and people went to his house to watch *him* watch the wrestling. He was a show in himself. He'd shout at the television and jump around like a madman. He kept trying to look up underneath the screen to see if the shoulders were pinned to the mat...He was one of the ones who choked to death.

And there was a wrestler in them days called "the Animal." *(VAL stands upstage left of the writing table.)* Remember that fella? The Animal! He had a rope around his neck, and they'd tie him on to the ring. Even the press fellas was afraid to talk to him. In fact, he couldn't talk. He could only grunt.

Yeah, the Animal. No name—just the Animal. No human being could beat him except Whipper Billy Watson, and that because Whipper Billy had such a pure heart.

I often wondered where the Animal lived, or what he did when he went home. I always reckoned he stayed over to his sister's, and when she'd come into a shop, people'd say *(whispering),* "That's the Animal's sister" while she'd be pickin' out a bone or a piece of raw gristle for his supper, and as the butcher'd wrap it up he'd say:

"A little something for the Animal, Miss Hawkins?" And she'd blush and nod, probably.

I daresay the Animal had a soft spot for her—his own sister after all. Or maybe she wasn't his sister at all—she only pretended, because she was in love with him. *(Very dramatic:)* A love that was never to be! *(He gets lost in it for a second.)* Oh, sorry, I'm gettin' all soppy. I'm watching too many soap operas on TV. That's another thing the cable's after doing for us. It's after bringin' a lot more very unhappy Americans into our living rooms. And I think I know why they're unhappy. Because their liquor cabinets are always full. *(Pause.)* They got nothing to strive for. Or maybe they're just cold. They got no clothes on most of the time.

Anyway, I got to run. I'm thinkin' about writin' a letter to the Animal. See if he'll come over and make Bernard change the channel. *(Thinking hard:)* Or maybe I should see if I can arrange a match between him and the Friendly Giant...give the youngsters something to think about... the Animal wouldn't be long smashing up that chair for two more to curl up in.

Or maybe I should let him have a go at Mr. Dressup. Oh well. Thanks again for the snaps.

Merry Christmas to all,

Yours,

Val

*As **VAL** puts the letter into an envelope and puts a stamp on it,* The Friendly Giant *theme music, "Early One Morning," starts. He lays the envelope on the table and puts on his winter coat, hat, and scarf from the coat tree on his right. He begins to walk across the front of the stage with his envelope in his hand. He is obviously going off to mail his letter. The music shortly blends into the* Mr. Rogers' Neighborhood *theme music as **UNCLE VAL** begins to walk through his neighbourhood. He stops downstage right and addresses the audience.*

VINCE MEETS THE BEATLES, BY UNCLE VAL

VAL: January 22, 1987

Dear Jack, I must admit, I'm beginning to find the suburbs more and more interesting. There's quite a few characters here. I don't know if the suburbs made them or if they were characters before they got here. There's an old fella down the road from us by the name of Vince, and he's a great friend of the Royal Family. He's an ordinary citizen in every other way. He can talk about the weather and the price of fish with the best of 'em. Then at a certain point he'll tell you how… Princess Margaret phoned him up just last night. Apparently, she's an awful bother to him. If she's not getting along with the queen or something, next thing you know, she'll be blubbering long-distance to Vince.

This puts quite a strain on his relationship with the queen and Prince Philip. They're much more reserved, apparently, than Princess Margaret. If they're not getting along, they won't come out and say it. But Vince can always tell. The queen will roll her eyes ever so slightly when Philip turns his back—just enough for Vince to get the message. Then he knows he's in for a night of it when Philip goes to bed. Apparently for the first hour or so the queen insists there's nothing wrong—but Vince eventually pries it out of her, she has a little cry, he makes her a cup of tea, and all is right with the Royals again.

> **VAL** *walks far stage left and, looking straight at the audience, he registers the cold by holding his sides and shivering; then he pulls an obvious black cord hanging from above. This somehow makes a burst of snow fall on his head and shoulders.*
>
> *Then, staying in place,* **VAL** *moonwalks towards stage left as the small, wall-mounted Canada Post letter box seems to be moving towards him. It is quite obviously attached to a black pole which someone backstage is manipulating; when the letter box reaches* **VAL***, he stops moonwalking and mails the letter. Then he turns around and, facing away from the letter box, moonwalks in the opposite direction, as the letter box recedes. He turns to the audience.*

VAL: Now, apparently, a lot of this happens—after hours—on the Royal Yacht *Britannia* when it's in St. John's harbour. After the dignitaries and the press go home, Vince will slip aboard—all the crew knows him— he'll go down to the queen's apartment and she'll be sitting there with her shoes off and her feet up on a worn-out old wingback chair.

> **VAL** *walks to the metal garbage can and sits on it—he is a little stage left of the doll's house.*

VAL: Now the thing that makes it so believable is that the whole thing is such a *burden* to him—and the details he goes into: like the picture he paints of himself bleary-eyed, coming down the gangplank in the wee hours, the sun rising over Cabot Tower, the burden of the empire off his shoulders for another day, hoppin' into a Bugden's taxi—hoping desperately that the cabbie won't notice that little regal hand *(does the waving hand then mimes a porthole and the queen looking out)* waving through the porthole.

Vince now is nearly ninety. He worked for one of the big merchants downtown all his life—behind the counter. Consequently, he's not exactly burdened with too much pension. So he only occasionally makes it over to Buckingham Palace these days.

Now there's never any mention in the papers of Vince *being* there— but then again, he shudders at the thought of publicity, and the Royal Family respect that. As do their guests.

Only the Beatles, he told me, stepped over the line, and after he met them at Buckingham Palace, they showed up on his doorstep in St. John's a few days later. He was sitting at his little chrome table when a knock come on the door *(he knocks on the roof of the doll's house, then stands, walks downstage and mimes opening the door)*; he opened it up and there was John, Paul, George, and Ringo with a bottle of rum.

He said he nearly had a heart attack.

But they were no trouble, he said. They had a few drinks and a little bit of lunch. Then they hired a taxi and went down to the Marine Drive. He said he had like to get mad at Ringo a few times for acting the fool, but in the end, he made him laugh in spite of himself.

"The Beatles," he told me, "just won't let you take yourself seriously."

I don't think he'd ever heard what happened to John, so I didn't bother to tell him. Anyway, they all went for a hamburger at the Pioneer Drive-In, and the Beatles were gone before he knew it.

I suppose the high and mighty would find a certain appeal in a man who spent his life in yard goods. Probably gives them a whole new perspective. I know he has a very calming effect on me. Some days it's awfully tempting to join him on one of those overseas flights. He hints at it from time to time.

But so far, my feet keep sticking to the ground. *(He gestures with fingers crossed on both hands.)*

So long, Jack, and love to all,

Val

As the Beatles sing "Her Majesty," **VAL** *walks to the chair at the kitchen table on stage left and drapes his coat and hat over it.*

JOEY SMALLWOOD ON MY MIND

ANDY: (*Moving the garbage can back to its place, he informally chats to the audience.*) I lived in Toronto for three years with my family from 1993 to 1996, and people there always figured I must really miss the peace and quiet of Newfoundland, where everything would be a lot more laid-back. I wanted to agree, but I realized the opposite was true. Life in Newfoundland and Labrador was *way* more intense. Being in Toronto was like a holiday.

At that time, the arts in Toronto seemed to exist far from the bigger political issues of the day. In the arts at home, it seemed our existence is always on the line. Our history and politics—even our geography—are daily issues. Everything is always on the edge...on the brink of crumbling...the edge of losing funding or the even crazier edge of continued underfunding—and all against that never-changing backdrop of losing more and more people to the mainland.

It seems like all of us have to worry about all of that all the time. To be a Newfoundlander is to be sentenced to a lifetime of worry. Even as a little tiny kid growing up in the suburbs, I can remember worrying about the fishery! Seriously!

I wonder, do children in Ontario worry about the Auto Pact? (Maybe they ought to.)

Also, as a kid...lying in my bunk bed on Rostellan Street, I remember hearing a report on the radio that there was apparently "no solution to the problem of potholes on Portugal Cove Road." (*He is frightened.*) NO SOLUTION! I worried about that for *years*.

And of course, my worries always seem to be accurate—the fishery is always in trouble, and Portugal Cove Road is still full of potholes.

It's all part of the "Burden of Being a Newfoundlander." Like, one time I remember being in Montreal taking a French course at the YMCA. It's the first class. Everyone's introducing themselves, and my turn is coming up, and I realize...I'm *blushing*. Because I know that I'm going to have to say I'm from *Newfoundland*, and I know that Newfie jokes are big in Quebec—I'd even seen them in the newspaper. This has never

AN EVENING WITH UNCLE VAL · 135

happened to me before. And I start thinking I gotta say that I'm from Newfoundland and then I got to speak *French. (With a passionate fear:)* What if I frig up?

When I'm touring across the country, the burden of my past is Joey Smallwood. He is always with me. His voice is in my ear.

JOEY SMALLWOOD: *(ANDY, doing his best Joey imitation, stands on the small soapbox/throne in the centre—it's a pulpit for Joey Smallwood's famous ranting oratorical style.)* Every time, every time, a Newfoundlander does *anything,* he represents Newfoundland. He is an ambassador for the province. If a Newfoundlander says something stupid, *Newfoundland* has said something stupid...and of course Labrador has also said something stupid... thus proving beyond a shadow of a doubt that we are incapable of governing ourselves! After which the federal authorities will quickly move in, dismantle the province, send in a colonial governor who, through a series of mass deportations, will turn our former country into a weather station with a staff of ten, and eventually of course even that will be moved to Halifax! *(Fervently:)* So for God's sake, Andy, do a good job on stage tonight. (**ANDY** *steps down from the soapbox/throne.)*

I TAKE THE BULLET FOR JFK

The lights slowly fade into a square in the middle of the stage. This square of light defines the "dressing room."

ANDY: Luckily, I have the Kennedys to encourage me. Jackie and JFK always show up in my dressing room after the show. Jackie always says *(in the soft, almost girlish voice of Jackie Kennedy:)* "Andy, we really loved your show." And I say, *(tearfully)* "Naw, it was no good. I'm thinking of quitting."

Then JFK says *(in an amazingly good JFK imitation!)* "Andy, listen, thousands of people see your shows. Don't let the Catholics down. Don't let the Pratts get ahead of you!"

The lighting quickly changes, so that he is in a narrower rectangle of light.

ANDY: Then suddenly, I'm sitting right between Jackie and JFK. We're in the back seat of the limousine in Dallas. I say...

Mr. President, could you tell the driver to put up the roof, or maybe speed up a little—then Kennedy says:

JFK: Andy, you must be ah, getting uncomfortable sitting on the ah, hump. Sit over here behind Governor Connally. *(He shifts to the right, as if he is changing places in the car.)*

ANDY: Kennedy moves over to the middle. I climb over Kennedy and sit behind Governor Connally when (**ANDY** *pulls out a starting pistol from his pocket and fires it twice in the air. Suddenly everything is in slow motion. The gun slowly undulates down until it is by the side of his head; he stares at the gun quizzically, then he suddenly mimes the bullet going into his own chest—he bends forward—then mimes being shot in the back—he bends backward. He collapses onto his knees. As he falls, he says matter-of-factly:)* Two gunmen. *(Now kneeling and still holding his chest, he says:)* I take the bullet for Kennedy—all of history is changed!

(He finally falls to the floor, realizes his head is out of the light, skitters back into the light for his big death scene.) Goodbye, my friends. The angels are coming for me. Hang on, are those angels? *(With a terrified gasp, he dies.)*

There is a blackout during which we hear sirens, panicked voices, then 1960s-style radio news-show music.

ANDY *(as pre-recorded voice of 1960s newscaster): (Still in the blackout)* And on the lighter side of the news, some people are saying the bullet in Dallas was meant for the president! Hahaha. *(He chuckles at this preposterous notion.)* That's it, good night.

1960s TV sign-off music fades as lights come up on **VAL**, *already seated at his desk.*

GOLD MEDAL AT THE SENIORS' OLYMPICS, BY UNCLE VAL

VAL: *(He is writing.)* February 3, 1987

Dear Jack, I'm home alone tonight babysitting for Jimmy and Kimmy. *(Looks up, stops writing.)* And the poodles. Margaret is in hospital. A new baby expected at any moment. So tonight at least I feel a little bit useful.

You mentioned in your letter that you were feelin' low because nobody ever asks you nuthin'.

I find the same thing, Jack. Oh, I mean people ask me things like, "How are you, old-timer?" Then they pat me on the head and walk away before I can answer.

I love that, as do all seniors. But I mean, nobody from the TV comes around asking me questions—and I got all the requirements: grey hair, no teeth, knobby hands.

Funny, because I see contemporaries of mine on TV with interviewers all agog with their stories of weather conditions in the 1920s, tales of caplin, early modes of courtship, et cetera. I find this line of questioning to my ah...colleagues a little tedious. One might almost say...boring. You notice I paused in front of the word "colleagues." I almost used those words: "senior citizens." Funny words. They seem to imply that you have attained a certain seniority in your citizenship. When in fact the opposite is true. "Junior Citizen" is more like it. "Grandfather, your Junior Citizen pension cheque has arrived!"

Like them "life certificates" we got to sign. You don't know about them yet, Jack, but once you start getting the old age pension, every so often you got to get a teacher or a doctor or a lawyer to sign a certificate that you're still alive! Oh yeah, it's so's no one can collect your pension after you're dead (a scheme I suspect Bernard is counting on). Yep! Just sign your name and know a teacher. That's all that's required to prove we're alive. Much easier than being a young person where you got to ride a skateboard or drive your friends to the edge of a wharf in a truck and yell, "The brakes are gone, the brakes are gone!"—or other such life-affirming activities.

No. No more of them good times required. *(Wistfully:)* No more dancin' 'til dawn or fallin' in love. No, it's just the eeeeeeeasy livin' of the St. John's senior. Like, take last winter, for example. Now that was a senior's delight. (*Stands at stage left of desk.*) Especially since we accidentally got the weather that was meant for Jupiter or some other planet!

I swear to God, if there were Senior Olympics, St. John's would be an event.

And the wind. The wind! Oh my, when you see them wispy old women being blown down Garrison Hill, you wonder there's not a special brigade struck for gaffin' them outta the harbour. Now there's an Olympic event right there. Bring your own pike pole and peavey. And then of course there's the hundred-yard dash to the Basilica in a sleet storm. Be good for that new young runner, whasisname? Ben Johnson.

And the dogs! The dogs have the key to the city of St. John's! Oh yeah. Ya meet dogs you know walking downtown.

—"Hello, Rex. Hello, Spot."

—"Morning, Uncle Val."

—"Promenading are ye boys?—Carry on!"

There's absolutely no sidewalk clearing. So if you *can* open your front door after a snowstorm, you got to brazen it out in the middle of the road with the dogs. Like running with the bulls at Pamplona. Tourists would pay to see that.

'Course the TV people are seldom interested in these realities. They want to get you crying into your beer about the good old days. Or blubbering about the big disasters. And they're so smirky, them TV people. "Well Skipper," they say, "do you think we're going to have a hard winter this year?" Smirk. Smirk. Like you might be a dogberry tree or something. I know what I'd say if they asked *me* that question.

I'd say, "It's going to be a rough winter for you, sir, without any legs." (*Slow:*) Then I'd threaten to have a go at his legs with an axe. (*He mimes the axe action.*) But of course, they never come around asking me questions. (*Walks towards desk. Turns around, looks back at audience.*) Must be the wild look in my eye...

(*He pauses. There is a passage of time. He pulls his chair out and sits.*) Well, it is sometime later now, Jack, and we have good news! The baby has been born. It's a boy. He is to be called Bradley. Bernard and I shared a drink. A first.

AN EVENING WITH UNCLE VAL • 139

Regards to all and please spread the good news far and wide. These…
glad tidings of great joy.

Val

VAL rises from the writing desk as the audience hears a recording of Ellen Power singing the Green's Harbour version of "While Shepherds Watch":

While shepherds watch
Their flocks by night
All seated on the ground.
The angel of the Lord came down,
The angel of the Lord came down,
And glory shone around.

As Ellen sings, VAL walks across to the doll's house on stage left. It rests on a large toy box.

He turns the house around, revealing the inside. It is a real doll's house, but the furniture and appliances are all painted on the walls. He reaches behind the toy box, picks up two five-inch dolls representing Bernard and Margaret. He stands them on the ground-floor level of the house. Then he finds a big-headed baby doll, which is in a wicker crib. He puts the baby doll and crib between the Bernard and Margaret dolls. They are, of course, stand-ins for Joseph, Mary, and the baby Jesus in the manger.

He then finds two Playmobil figures who are holding hands. They represent Jimmy and Kimmy. Two tiny identical white stuffed animals represent the poodles Tiffy and Tuffy. He puts them around the edge of this Christmas nativity scene as if they are the visitors and the animals around the manger in Bethlehem.

Finally, he reaches down and picks up a knitted tourist version of a fisherman in yellow rubber coveralls—this represents himself. He puts this in the nativity scene.

He pulls a tiny cord and, as happened to VAL himself earlier, snow falls on the baby Jesus/Bradley. A sharp beam of divine light illuminates the baby.

When this little Christmas interlude is completed, **VAL** *walks to the chrome kitchen table on extreme stage left; he picks up the teapot, pours himself a steaming hot cup of tea. He then holds it up towards the audience as if it is a chalice to be consecrated.*

"ODE TO TEA," BY UNCLE VAL

VAL: *(In his sincerest dramatic, heartfelt poet's voice:)* "Ode to Tea," by Valentine Reardigan
Clothed in a beautiful hot cup
you cry out
you beg
for the cool, creamy juice of the cow
to be released from its metal
Carnation prison *(He picks up the can of Carnation condensed milk and
pours it with a strong flow and a wide arc into the tea.)*
and how jauntily you invite the playful sugar crystals
to mingle *(He puts a spoonful of sugar in the tea.)*
to mix *(He stirs in the sugar.)*
to die!...And *live again*—
in your tannic fluidity.
Oh tea, oh my tea, *(looking lovingly into the cup)*
Bernard's pocket calculator tells me
that up to yesterday
I've drunk
five hundred and forty-four thousand,
seven hundred and eleven cups of you.
And yet I love you more than the very first time ever I brought you
into the house
Who
I ask you
can say that
of their spouse?

AN EVENING WITH UNCLE VAL • 141

VAL *bows, takes a good sip of tea, and walks to the lower stack of boxes at centre stage—talking as he walks.*

SHAKESPEARE IN THE BURBS, BY UNCLE VAL

VAL: April 23, 1987

Dear Jack, Good news. I've finally come into my own in St. John's. I've decided to throw my lot in with the cultural revival crowd and write a play. (**VAL** *is now at the stage right of the lower stack of cardboard boxes. As he talks, he removes his jacket, he places it behind a box, and, unseen by the audience, he puts on his poodle slippers.*) I thought you should be the first to read it. I have enclosed the first scene, (*he reaches behind the boxes and retrieves a Spider-Man cape, which he puts on; he walks behind the lower stack of boxes*) which, for reasons that will become apparent, I cannot show to Bernard or Margaret. It's a kind of a Shakespeare murder mystery.

(*Having now disappeared behind the boxes, he shouts his introduction:*) Act one. Scene one. A house. By a heath. Not that far from the Avalon Mall.

(*He enters from the other side of the lower stack of boxes, narrating as he goes.*) Enter Prince Val, a hunchback, with two poodles. (*Making a bad royal fanfare trumpet sound:*) Brrpp brrpp a-pa-brrpp brrpp brrpp brrrrrp (*repeat to taste*).

Having entered to his own fanfare, **VAL** *is now on stage left of the lower stack of boxes. He is wearing fluffy white poodle slippers. He is bent over as the crippled prince; he uses his hand to make a hump on his back. He backs up until the poodles are close to centre stage. Then he slips the poodles off his feet. They are attached to monofilament which leads off stage.*

VAL: Stay! (*The poodles move a tiny bit*). I said "stay." (*They move a bit, then stop.*)

VAL: (*as hunchback* **PRINCE VAL**): (*Walking down towards the audience, he speaks in an intimate, famous-Shakespearian-soliloquy style.*) St. John's is quiet tonight. A mantle of new fall'n snow (*he removes his hand from the hump position and gestures with it towards the snow that has fallen in the "Vince Meets* *the Beatles" scene)* blankets its curious winding streets and its ranch-style suburban housing units. Only the occasional war-whoop of neighbourhood children shatters the chilly stillness. *(He is pacing now.)* Bernard is downstairs in the rec room, blind drunk and speechless. Jimmy, Kimmy, and Bradley have chest colds and are bedridden and heavily sedated, the rhythmic rattle of their tiny chests providing a pleasant counterpoint to the dull monotony of their humidifier. *(He's proud of having written that line. He bows quickly. He walks back to the poodles.)* Two noble hounds of the ancient poodle breed lie snoring at my feet, their stomachs distended from their royal portions of table scraps. *(Quickly:)* Margaret is at a PTA meeting.

(He moves downstage again, taking the audience into his confidence.) I am, for this brief period, master of all I survey, *(picks up a cheap plastic child's tiara from behind the toy box and puts it on)* new-crowned King of the Kitchen, Lord of the Living room, Baron of the Bathroom. *(Secretive:)* My only enemy is the evil King Bernard in the basement. But at this very moment he is not prepared for war. My spies have told me this. Should I attack now and risk my kingdom, or wait for the warlike Lady Margaret to return from the PTA meeting? It is certain—my spies have told me— that they will do battle tonight. King Bernard is bound to be wounded, winged, routed, crushed. Hahahaha...But drat my luck—he will rise again tomorrow morning as he always does, to lead his evil empire once again. *(He pivots histrionically, then sits on the soapbox/throne, imitating* The Thinker. *He thinks dramatically.)*

Yes! I must move tonight. I will challenge him to a duel!!!—waking the wheezing children as our seconds. His drunkenness and my advanced years will make for an even match. But hark! The Lady Margaret comes. I hear the drums of war contain-èd in her shout. I must take off...this plastic crown *(he struggles to remove the plastic tiara as if it is very weighty)*...and put on my jester's gear. *(From one of the boxes, he pulls out a large Christmas stocking, which he wears as a jester's hat with bells.)* Enter the queen.

Ah! Lady Margaret!

The King is in the basement in his cups.

And I am here alone with these noble poodle pups.

AN EVENING WITH UNCLE VAL • 143

Exit the queen in a rage, the poodles in pursuit.

The poodle slippers are pulled off stage awkwardly by monofilament; it's not quite working. **VAL** *encourages them.*

VAL: Go on! Git! Git! *(They finally are clumsily jerked out.)* Hahahaha! Now I'll to the basement, hide behind a curtain and witness Bernard's rout.
(He becomes serious.) But my plans for revenge must
For a while be put to sea.
And so as not to show
The cowardly quaking of my knee, *(His knees quake and shimmy.)*
I'll innocent-like put on the kettle *(He grabs a teacup.)*
And have a cup of tea...*He makes trumpet sounds and drinks tea triumphantly.)*
Brrpp brrpp a-pa-brrpp brrpp brrpp brrrrrp!

Very dramatic timpani drums end the scene as the electric kettle boils madly on the table. It fades into a loudly whistling kettle.

Blackout.

PARLIAMENT OF CULTURAL ROMANCE

Lights up. Once again, **ANDY** *is found lying on the floor in the "dressing room" light area. It has the same lighting as in his previous "I Take the Bullet for JFK" scene. It's* **ANDY**'s *Dallas death pose.*

ANDY: *(Waking up on the floor of his dressing room.)* I wake up. *(Holds his hands to his chest, checking for blood; he is disappointed.)* Aww. I didn't take the bullet for Kennedy. History unfolds as it was previously reported. I'm still in my dressing room. I'm on tour...There's a bunch of Newfoundlanders there; they are all living in Toronto or Calgary or wherever I'm performing, and they're all homesick, so I get to go out for a beer with them after the show. And Joey Smallwood comes along, of course. And the Kennedys. Sir William Coaker usually shows up after the gay bars close (even the gay bars close early in Calgary), and Pope John XXIII is there, and Cavendish Boyle and Noel Dinn and Neil Murray…and look! Marilyn Monroe is over there, seated at a table—deep in conversation with JFK. Oh, and Jackie's there too, she's seated at another table and she's talking to someone. My God, it's Bob Marley! Noel Dinn and John Lennon are arguing about the seal hunt. Dinn is against; Lennon is in favour *(moves garbage can into "dressing room" light).*

Then my mother and father come over to my table. Mom's worried about me doing material about the family on stage, and Dad says, "For God's sake, Agnes, shur he's got nothing. No offence, Andy—I'm glad you got a focus in your life—but the Arts! Jeez, even I had a pension."

And I say, "Dad, I haven't got *nothing.* I've got a house, a car, a washer and a dryer." And Mom says, "Yes, but there's your old classmate Danny Williams with 243 million dollars."

Dad says, "That's exactly my point, Andy. Any material you want to do about me—go right ahead, as long as it turns a buck." (**ANDY** *sits wearily on the garbage can.)* "Shur there's nothing left of me now anyway except a few bones and this old tweed jacket you buried me in. And stop looking at me like that, Andy—no, there is no life after death—I'm being generated by your brain."

Then Mom says, "Well I don't know about that, Michael."

Then Dad says, "For God's sake, Agnes, don't get him started," and we all spend the whole night together—the whole crowd of us—drinking deep from the restorative waters of that great narrative river that flows through the hearts and souls of all the people from Newfoundland and Labrador. And their friends from "away" who know there is something special about this place, or that at least…Once upon a time, there was a special place. Not in my time or in your time, but in times long ago. In pod auger days when quart bottles held half a gallon, houses were papered with pancakes, and pigs run about with forks stuck in their ass seein' who wanted a slice of ham.

And what an exciting time it was. *(The "dressing room" lights cross-fade as full lights are restored across the stage. We are out of the "dressing room" now.)*

It was the seventies! And we were actors, and writers and musicians, and filmmakers and poets and painters. At least I think we were because we were actually doing it—despite the skeptical looks of...well, pretty well everybody.

Our job was to tell the story of what it is to be human through the telling of *our story,* through the celebration of our great cultural narrative, poking at it, exposing it, laughing at it, debating it, adapting and retelling it—in order to bring the audiences to...tears *and* to laughter—to their knees—and sometimes to their feet about it *and* because of it.

We wanted to learn everything about Newfoundland and Labrador.

(Moves garbage can downstage; sits on it.) Ladies and gentlemen, in 1977 I was fortunate to be one of a group of people who attended the wedding of Anita Best to Pius Power Jr. in South East Bight in Placentia Bay. It was a turning point.

Anita would, of course, go on to be one of our most famous singers and folklorists, but that day in 1977, she was marrying the son of Mr. Pius Power Sr., the great teller of the Newfoundland Jack tales.

(He moves the metal garbage can back in place.) I'd never even heard of the Jack tales, other than the one about the guy who climbed the beanstalk and the other guy who was every inch a sailor and the one who jumped over the candlestick.

But now of course everyone knows all about Jack, so I won't go goin' on about Jack. I won't tell you how Jack married the princess, how he flew across the ocean in a magic punt, how he beat the devil's grandmother at a game of Chinese checkers, *(sits on centre box/throne)* how he used his magic powers to make the world stand still, then he got off and changed a tire, how one time he had a thousand women in love with him for a forty-eight-hour period, how he wrestled an elephant, how he ballet-danced with a frog, how he sword-fought the entire provincial cabinet...how he was discovered to be a woman, how the woman-Jack was discovered to be a man again, how he was swallowed by a whale, how he never climbed the beanstalk at all, and how, disguised as Jupiter, he attended the planets' annual soup supper and dance...because I know you know all about that.

ANDY *switches to* UNCLE VAL*'s voice and Job's Cove accent.)*

VAL: I won't tell you about how, when he was a young man, all he ever done was sit around in the coal box all day long. Oh yeah, he never washed his face and never combed his hair and never shaved 'til he was twenty-one years of age—all he ever done was take a potato, cut a hole in it, stick it on his big toe, stick it in the fire, roast it, and eat it. And that's how the young Jack spent his time.

ANDY *returns to his own voice.*

ANDY: And there I was, listening to this story in Mr. Pius Power's house, which was built on sticks over the ocean (it was *in* the ocean, we'll say), and I was practically sitting in that coal box. I could see the part of the stove that opened up for the potato on the toe. And of course, young Pius was Jack, and Anita Best was the princess, and the royal wedding supper was served in shifts...'cause there were 200 people to be fed in a tiny outport kitchen and since I'd put in all that time worryin' about the fishery, I was glad to see it was alive and well there in South East Bight.

That great three-day wedding was the intersection of everything that we held dear. The singers, the actors, the folklorists, the fishermen, the friends, the storytellers were all at the same event, all accents, all classes.

It was...the Parliament of Cultural Romance...all aided by just enough rum to keep a buzz on. After three days, the Parliament adjourned, and we all went down the road to discover and report on the riches of our culture—to mine them and then share the wealth—but I was this young fella from the suburbs of St. John's, so I thought, "My God, how can I get in on this?"

PARLIAMENT OF CULTURAL ROMANCE: TOWNIE IMPOSTER

ANDY: I mean, I knew nothing about the fishery—in fact I was deathly afraid of the water, especially afraid of what was underneath the water. I just didn't want to know what was going on down there. Kind of like the federal Department of Fisheries in that way, I guess. When I was a little kid, I used to go down to St. Philip's, an outport near St. John's, and stand on the wharf for hours and hours and watch the fishermen *(he mimes the fishermen's actions)* split the fish, tear the heads off, throw them in the water, *(repeats:)* split the fish, tear the heads off, throw them in the water, and after a while at the bottom there'd be this huge mass of cods' heads rolling back and forth on the bottom looking up at me with accusing eyes, like: *(He does his "codfish face" by sticking out his jaw and his bottom lip: with the jaw protruding, the bottom lip comes back to touch the top lip, making a puckering sound; all the while, his eyes dart back and forth in googly cod style as his extended hand undulates in front of him like the tail of a fish. This codfish moment is accompanied by a quiet recording of a part of Shostakovich's* Jazz Suite No. 2, Waltz No. 2.*)*

Then later on we'd go swimming in that same water, and I'd be swimming along on top of the cods' heads *(he does the breaststroke),* and I could hear them calling me down! *(He becomes the calling dead cod, his arms reaching up, trying to grab the little suburban boy swimming above.)* "Come down, come down, Andy, and taste the putrescent fruits of death!" *(**ANDY** looks down at the heads below while his arms are still swimming the breaststroke. Then he looks up in horror and quickly swims away.)* "No, thanks! I'm from the suburbs! I'm here as part of a purely recreational event!"

The Shostakovich music rises to a low crescendo. Lost in the moment, **ANDY** *continues his sublime breaststroke dance until the music fades out. Then he pulls himself together.*

ANDY: Of course, Uncle Val was the solution!

I was able to talk about what I knew best: the suburbs of St. John's. But have it come straight from the horse's mouth.

Anyway, I just bring all this up to put things in context for the Danes here this evening. *(He looks pityingly towards any confused Danish people in the audience, then walks slightly stage right of centre and, without sitting, he starts a new letter.)*

MAULED AT THE TEDDY BEARS' PICNIC, BY UNCLE VAL

VAL: Dear Jack,

Well, I'm in trouble with Margaret. I'm after frightening the life outta the youngsters with one of me stories. Since Bradley's born, I been tucking the older tykes in at night and tellin' them the odd tale to help them in their voyage to dreamland. The other night we got to talkin', and they asked me, "Where do babies come from?"

Well, I was taken aback. But I decided to take the bull by the horns and just tell them straight out that they had been brought up by wolves... and that I had found them while out settin' me rabbit slips. This meant I had to tell them that the woods out behind the suburbs are just teemin' with wolves and that I was in regular contact with them.

They seemed quite interested. Which led to my wolf howl demonstration. And I guess I got carried away—especially when I did my wolf face for them. You know my wolf face, Jack. (**VAL** *picks up his reading glasses from the writing table and sticks the lens parts into the flesh below his lower eyelids, making his eyes pop out in a scary way.*)

Anyway, they soon started in whimperin' and it was four o'clock in the morning before they closed their saucer-sized eyes. Neither of them have been alone since. They have to be accompanied to the bathroom, the bedroom, upstairs, downstairs, inside or out. And not by me. Every time I offer to help, they whimper (*in a high-pitched child's voice:*) "No, you might turn into a wolf again."

So here I sit, exiled to my room until the wolf scare passes. (*He sits at the writing table.*)

Now in my day that was one of the prime reasons for tellin' stories. Old fellas used to come over and sit around the kitchen and frighten the youngsters rigid. For some people in the community, this was actually their calling. (*He stands.*) Like, there was always that story of the fella who—when he was alive—had struck his own mother and when he died, his hand kept rising up in the coffin like this (*he demonstrates the hand snapping up from the elbow, and he makes a few attempts to push it down—but it keeps rising up again*) so they had to put a little wooden tower onto the coffin to accommodate the hand *(he mimes the tower over the upright arm)*.

There was a lot more problems with corpses in those days. They were a lot less cooperative on the whole; there were always people who wouldn't stay in their coffins at night because it was too cold, so they'd slip into bed with one of the living; there were bodies that sat up in their coffins—that seemed to happen an awful lot, and it seemed like most corpses *moaned* at least once or twice, and the dead were forever tappin' on walls, appearin' at windows, ridin' on white horses, warning people of this or that. Oh yeah, they were very busy, the older-time dead. The younger generation of dead must be on drugs or something. They're very lackadaisical. Or maybe they're just more polite since we joined Confederation.

And the Old Hag seems to have retired. You never hear of her anymore. She must be gettin' her Canada Pension; the woods have been cleared of fairies, banshees, boo darbies, visions. People still *talk* about the devil, but nobody ever *meets* him anymore; how many stories did you used to hear of people having the longest kind of a chat with a handsome, well-dressed stranger—then they look down and see he had…cloven hoofs! That was always the scariest part of the story, when they'd see them hoofs *(he shivers deeply)* ooooohhh!—then the devil would disappear in a ball of fire!

That don't happen no more—not even to the TV evangelists. 'Course I wouldn't be surprised if some of them got hoofs.

Since I grew up in that kind of a world, I couldn't see how a few talkin' wolves would upset Jimmy and Kimmy. 'Specially suburban wolves. And you *can* talk to them y'know, Jack. Oh yes, all you got to do is go to the edge of the woods in the middle of the night and call out *(he shouts as if into the woods)* "Hello, wolf! It's a lonely world, wolf!" And they'll come out and talk to you.

But are they wolves, Jack? Or are they old men like you and me who turn into wolves at night and cry for their lost youth and their lost loved ones?

*(***VAL*** goes feral. He whoops.)* Aroooooooooooooooooooooooo! YipYipYipYip Yip! Aroooooooooooooooooooooo!

As **VAL** *does his "scary glasses face," wild drumming music fills the room. This causes the whooping* **VAL** *to dance with abandon over to the boxes behind him. Still dancing, he picks up a cloak made of fake-fur animal skins—including some old-fashioned women's fox-fur stoles. It also has a hood with a child's stuffed dog attached to it. He puts on the cloak and hood. He dances over to the metal garbage can. He drums on the top of it.*

(An accordion version of "Mussels in the Corner" begin to blend in with the drumming. **VAL**, *the feral wolf dancer, hears it. It sends him into a square-dancing trance; he first step-dances in place, then dances down towards the audience, dipping his head down as if going under an opposite dancing couple. He then does "hand over hand" towards stage right, then "hand over hand" towards stage left. He step-dances sideways to centre stage. Finally, he puts his arm around an imaginary dancer for "swing your partner." He spins madly. He step-dances some more until, exhausted, he sits on the centre soapbox/throne. He takes off the wolf's head and hide.)*

VAL: Hmmm. I guess I *did* get a bit carried away. Anyway, I'm sure they'll soon be over it, and in a few years, they'll be ready for the *corpse stories.* I'm lookin' forward to that.

If I'm not one myself by then.

MEET MY MENTOR, FRANCIS COLBERT

ANDY: Ladies and gentlemen, I always hope these letters are somewhere in the Newfoundland recitation tradition, which my generation were at the tail end of. Uncle Val has good credentials as a reciter, because he's based on my imitation of Francis Colbert.

Francis Colbert, if you never got to see him or if you're from Denmark, was a great reciter and storyteller from Job's Cove in Conception Bay.

I watched him first perform at the Good Entertainment Festival in Killdevil, on the west coast of Newfoundland in 1978—and I was totally blown away by this really rare *presence* he had on stage. Actually, backstage I'd see him standing around—he seemed very frail (**ANDY** *takes a*

AN EVENING WITH UNCLE VAL • 151

pose like the older Francis Colbert, slightly bent over with his fingers in cigarette-holding position) and he always had a cigarette in his hand, and I remember thinking, "This poor old guy—they won't even be able to *hear* him on stage"—but once he got in front of the audience he transformed. He did all the standard Newfoundland recitations, like *St. Peter at the Gate, Lobster Salad,* and *The Smoke Room on the Kyle.* He was obviously very familiar with the works of Robert Service, but he also wrote his own recitations.

This is my imitation of Francis doing a poem that he wrote called "The Ballad of Job's Cove Rock." So, like, first he'd be backstage looking kinda frail…*(Imitating a feeble Francis with a soft quavering voice:)* "I think they called my name, Andy."

> **ANDY** *slowly climbs up on the soapbox/throne as if very shaky and frail then he takes a recitation pose and bursts forth powerfully. He uses lots of hand gestures, in the old tradition.*

FRANCIS COLBERT: There's a fishing spot called Job's Cove Rock,
And it lies in Conception Bay.
Men fished its shoals,
God rest their souls;
They are long since passed away.
Yet memory lingers ever on:
As stars they once shone bright,
Men who fished on Job's Cove Rock,
Where the big ones always bite.

ANDY: This is a true story of Francis and two of his friends who very, very nearly get lost in the fog out on Conception Bay. They actually end up just off Baccalieu Island. My favourite part of the poem is where they think that they're not going to make home again and they make a pact.

FRANCIS COLBERT: Then Ned turns to me
And "Frank," says he,
"We're doomed this time, I guess.

I think we're down below the grounds
So we'll head her up sou'west.
But there's one request I'd like to make"—
And his voice seemed low and weak—
"That if you're about when I pass out,
Just dump me in the deep."
Well, he seemed so low,
I couldn't say no,
So I said, "I will agree,
But if you survive
And I'm not alive
Just do the same for me."

ANDY: Actually, I got to know Francis Colbert at that Festival at Killdevil and eventually became good friends with him, and he stayed with us on Pennywell Road whenever he came in for the folk festival. And eventually he was in the feature film we made called *The Adventure of Faustus Bidgood*, which I'm going to show right now. (*Lights dim for the movie.*) Only kidding. (*Lights come back.*) It's three hours long. (**ANDY** *wipes his forehead in relief and looks at his watch.*)

So we spent a lotta time together, me and Francis. He was a fascinating guy. I always remember him telling me that he could recall a time before he had an engine in his boat and he had to *row* out to his cod traps on Conception Bay. When he told me that, sitting there at my little chrome table on Pennywell Road, I felt like I was on a subcommittee of the Parliament of Cultural Romance.

That's where I also learned about silences. Usually, I'm not comfortable unless there's constant chattering. But with me and Francis, there were always long, long, silences…and I got used to them. We'd mostly sit at the kitchen table and smoke…cigarettes…together…there'd be a long, silence…and after a while, Francis'd say, (*quietly*) "Cigarette, Andy?"

And I'd say "Ahhhh…yeah, okay, I'll have one of yours, Francis. Yeah. Yeah." We'd smoke away, smoke away…then after a while I'd say, "Cigarette, Francis?"

He'd say, *(like it was something he'd never thought of before)* "Ah...yeah, I'll have one of yours, Andy." Every now and then, he'd change his mind and he'd say, "No, no, I think I'll have one of my own."

And we smoked the same brand of cigarettes. And we had the same *number* of cigarettes. It was very calming.

He was a very dry and witty man, but also quite mysterious. Sometimes he'd just say strange things out of the blue. One day he just said, out of nowhere *(in a reverie)* "I hates carrots. I hates the thought of 'em even growing in the ground." Once, I asked him if he ever smoked dope. "Yeees," he said. "A fella come down to the club one time with some marijuana and he said 'If you have one puff of this,' he said, 'it's the same as drinkin' three dozen beer.'"

I said, "Whoa! Did it affect you?"

"Nawww, it had no effect on me," he said. "'Course then again, neither does three dozen beer."

A recording of the "Portuguese Waltzes" is played by Duane Andrews on the guitar as **ANDY** *announces the intermission.*

~ *INTERMISSION* ~

PART TWO

The set is slightly altered. The doll's house has been turned around, and once again the front of the house faces the audience. The writing desk is gone. It has been replaced by a pile of furniture and an additional cardboard box. A white plastic beef bucket is now slightly stage right of the lower stack of boxes. The large metal garbage can has been moved farther stage left and downstage. One of the chrome chairs is at the downstage side of the kitchen table and faces the audience. A colourful blanket is draped over the back of this chair. There is a music box and a baby's rattle on the kitchen table.

LOVE IN THE TIME OF COLIC, BY UNCLE VAL

ANDY *in his own street clothes enters stage right; he talks informally to audience.*

ANDY: Welcome back, ladies and gentlemen, to the second half of *An Evening with Uncle Val.* As we start Part Two of our saga, we find our hero, Uncle Val, firmly ensconced in the *suburbs!* For a long time, it seemed like a bad dream. Surely he will awake on his daybed next to the coal box, next to the stove in his *own* kitchen, and yet...(*pointing to the teapot*) a cup of tea at the suburban kitchen table is still a cup of tea.

(*He walks downstage left to the kitchen chair that is facing the audience. He takes a blanket off the back of it and sits with the blanket on his lap.*)

And even though he is a bayman, he must admit the harbour of St. John's is as good a harbour as any in that land, despite the sewerage bubble. Val tries to find a way to ignore the family and drift off with the noise and chaos around him. And so he tries to pull the covers up over his head...(**ANDY** *pulls the blanket up over his head.*) But the cries of that colicky baby (*he pulls blanket off his head*), that insistent little Bradley, keep them all awake for three whole weeks, 'til one night Val gets up, goes in

AN EVENING WITH UNCLE VAL • 155

to Margaret and says…(**ANDY** *gets up suddenly and pulls the blanket off, then, reaching out his arms into the darkness of offstage left, in* **VAL**'s *voice, he says:*)

VAL: Give him to me, Margaret! Give him to me! Give him to me before you throw him out the window.

> *The arms of the assistant stage manager can barely be seen passing a "baby" to* **VAL**, *who receives the swaddled baby in the blanket he is holding.*

VAL: I'll walk it out of him. (*Having wrapped the baby in the blanket in his arms, he walks back and forth.*)
Like my own grandfather done for me, so the story goes, down on the landwash, put to sleep by the jagged lullaby of the beach rocks underfoot.

ANDY: (*Still rocking the baby in his arms:*) And Val does the same thing for Bradley on the crushed stone of the suburban driveway. And so greatness is thrust upon our hero from a most unexpected place. As he was heard to say:

VAL: (*Hugging the baby tightly*) Like some great colossus I have spanned the era of the open dory and the era of the disposable diaper—quite a number of which I have changed, by the way, something I never did for me own youngsters.

> **VAL** *continues speaking as he walks stage left and places the baby-bundle on a changing table behind the curtain—just out of sight of the audience. He makes baby-changing gestures behind the curtain, pulls a used diaper out, and throws it into the metal garbage can.*

VAL: Well, I wanted a job and now I got one: full-time babysitter for little Bradley. I am officially no longer as useless as the poodles. (*To the baby, who is falling asleep offstage:*) Shhhh. (*Speaking just above a whisper to the audience as he sits back in the kitchen chair:*)

In fact (and this is confidential, Jack), my next-door neighbour Celia has been dropping in to visit me regularly. I know I swore when Louise died I would never "couple" again, but Celia is quite lovely…plump…outgoing, very witty. She had similar eye surgery to mine, and Margaret got us together. A relationship founded on sore eyes got nowhere to go but up.

Now don't go mentionin' me and Celia to the crowd out home or they'll just jump to conclusions, like poor Vince did when he seen us sittin' on the back bridge together. He was over in a flash reciting his poetry about royal weddings, all of which are *happy* apparently. *(**VAL** looks to the stage left baby area as if he has heard something.)* Uh-oh. Bradley's stirring. *(He picks up a baby rattle and a music box from kitchen table, winds up the music box and walks towards the offstage baby area.)* Bernard and Margaret are out to a do somewhere. I was two and a half hours putting Bradley to sleep—even though he was plimmed to the gills with milk. *(He listens closely where he just left baby Bradley.)* Wait. No. *(Whispering:)* He's gone back to sleep. *(He walks back to the kitchen table and puts back down the music box and the rattle.)* Oh yes, Jack, I forgot to mention…Celia is after convincing me to take a course up to the University! Yeah. I didn't know it was possible. It's a folklore seminar. I suspect I will be Exhibit A.

The lights fade, and the audience hears a recording of the "Portuguese Waltzes" played by Duane Andrews on the guitar. The lights come back up on the downstage centre left dressing room area—where we last saw **ANDY** *talking to President Kennedy.*

CUBIST THEATRE

ANDY: I'm in my dressing room. I'm on tour. This time I really *am* in Denmark. And there are a bunch of Danes there, and they're upset because I keep going off the topic, and I tell them I do that in all my shows and that I used to feel bad about it until I realized…that it's "cubist theatre." You know how Picasso shows you all sides of an image, even the ones you shouldn't be able to see from that particular angle. Well, I'm doing the same thing. I'm just flattening out my brain for you…

Let me illustrate. *(From inside one of the boxes piled up behind him, he gets a set of tall cardboard divider panels used to separate six tall glass objects during shipping.)*

Let's say this is my brain. *(He shows the dividers from every angle.)* So what I'm doing is…I'm flattening out my brain. *(He pulls the dividers apart and flattens them across his chest. The dividers directly in front of his chest bend easily in three sections: right, middle, and left.)* I'm allowing you to see this totally unrelated thought *(pointing to the right section)* that just happens to be lodged right next to the current topic of conversation right here. *(Pointing to the adjacent middle section.)* And let's face it, this *(indicating the right section)* is usually much more interesting.

For example this *(the middle section)* is the housewife discussing new oven fuses with Gerry, the repairman…and this *(pointing to the unrelated adjacent right section)* is the housewife's fantasy of making passionate love to Gerry on the kitchen floor. So—I'm going to deny you this *(points to unrelated right section)* because of some academic idea of what a play is!?

No, my friends, I am free of that. You too can be free. *(Svengali:)* Just follow me. *(Accompanied by a heavenly harp decrescendo sound, he draws the audience in with come-hither gestures and says eerily:)* Come into my world… *(He then puts the cardboard back into the box.)*

I TAKE THE BULLET FOR JFK, PART TWO: BOB MARLEY & JACKIE O

ANDY: And then JFK comes into my dressing room. He's alone, so I ask him the question I have always wanted to ask him, even though it's off the topic…I say:

How about you? Like, *all those women!* How could a Catholic boy like you feel free to act like that? And Kennedy says:

JFK: I ah, felt ah, sort of ah, like I was *above the law*…I guess I was too privileged…

ANDY: Yet—you were so moral on stuff like civil rights…

JFK: Yes, but that is not *personal* morality; that is *public* morality, leadership morality, righting old wrongs, trying to make life more bearable for a greater and greater number of people.

ANDY: I say, "Yeah, well, what about Marilyn?"

JFK: I ah, made life unbearable for her. I broke her heart. Because ah, you see, I fooled myself. I told myself that I was such an important and powerful person that she just had to be fulfilled. I would not face the fact that it was a complex situation, that the act of making love draws energy from the heart and it can only be restored by real love.

ANDY: Then Marilyn Monroe comes into the dressing room, puts her arms around him. JFK says:

JFK: But Andy, we are ah, together now.

ANDY: And I say, "What about Jackie?"

JFK: Oh, Jackie. Oh ah, Jackie's fine. She's ah, with Bob Marley. They're great together. She's dropped that ah, whole upper-class New England thing. Yeah, they get along just swell.

> *As the lights fade on the dressing room area, we hear a recording of Bob Marley from his 1978 song "Is This Love."*

DEATH—REAL AND IMAGINED,
BY UNCLE VAL

VAL: (*Sits on the soapbox/throne*) Sad news. Poor old Vince down the road died on Friday. I told you about Vince a number of times, I know. His daughter said he died happy, because even though he hadn't been to visit the Royal Family for quite some time, the Beatles (he told her) had dropped in to see to him just last week. I didn't see the Beatles at the

AN EVENING WITH UNCLE VAL • 159

funeral home, but I was sure they'd been there, so I took the liberty of signing their names in the book.

VAL *goes to the chrome table and pours a cup of already steeped tea from the teapot.*

VAL: Margaret and Bernard seemed quite depressed by Vince's passing. 'Course I find all the heavy sighing and staring into the void a bit hard to take. I mean, I could go at any minute. I no longer even require a "cause of death." I can just *stop*.

A kind of senior crib death. And the laws of nature and the wheel of fortune have already determined the exact time and place. *I* just don't happen to know yet. It may be during some insignificant moment, like while promising myself not to forget to buy razor blades in the morning. Then poof! I'm an organ donor. I might have time for one last observation like "Golly it seems dark all of a sudden, I wonder if we're having a power fa—" and the rest is dot, dot, dot. *(He moves to the area behind the doll's house.)*

Or I might be running up a hill, marvelling at my invincibility, picturing myself for one burning moment as a well-oiled machine—when suddenly I seize up, cough out a vital organ, and find myself floating over the house. *(He hovers over the doll's house, arms outstretched like soaring eagle's wings.)*

Listening to Margaret inside the house fretting *(looking in through the back of the doll's house)* and saying, "I don't know where he could be; it's not like him not to call."

And Bernard with his head buried in the paper replying, *(looking up at the audience; drops eagle's wings as he imitates Bernard looking into paper)* "Whaaaaaat?"

And Margaret sayin', "You're not listening to me, now Bernard, are you?" And they'll break into a fight and forget about me *(he stretches out his arms and "floats" again)* 'til my organs are well past transplant potential. *(He moves to downstage right of the doll's house.)*

Or maybe I'm going right now! *(Slight panic in his voice)* And that's why I'm thinking this way. Perhaps the last sentence I just said is the second-last sentence of my life. *(Beat; he waits...)*

Nope, I guess not. *(He moves back to chrome table, adds milk and sugar to his tea, and picks up the cup.)*

I was kinda hopin' it *was*. So I wouldn't have to look at them long faces on Bernard and Margaret. *(Takes a sip of tea; then he has an idea! He moves closer to the doll's house, crouches down, and looks in through the back of it.)*

Or maybe I should sneak out the back window and visit Celia. *(He stands up.)* Maybe we could elope. Now that'd be the way to die, on our honeymoon, locked together in a moment of septuagenarian ecstasy. Two package-tour seniors loved to death in Niagara Falls. Cause of death: life.

So long, Jack. And so long to Vince *(holds cup of tea up as a toast to Vince)*— fount of Royal Knowledge, poet, and gentleman. You're no doubt up there right now, Vince, havin' the longest kind of a chat to John Lennon. And I am sure that John Lennon is up there—despite what they're sayin' about him lately, wha? Oh my...I'm not so sure about Picasso, though. But far be it from me to judge—since I'm probably only a chest cold away from judgment myself.

So long, Jack.

A recording of John Lennon's "Whatever Gets You thru the Night" fades in.

75 CANDLES: VAL'S BIRTHDAY, BY UNCLE VAL

*As **VAL** begins to speak, he walks over to the pile of furniture stage right, where the writing desk was in the first half of the show. He picks up a Canadian Tire shopping bag that is on top of the pile of furniture.*

VAL: Thanks to you and Madonna for the birthday card. It arrived yesterday morning, right on time. *(He walks over and sits on the middle soapbox/throne.)* It was an eventful day, my birthday. Bernard came into my room at seven a.m., dancing a jig and waving a gift certificate. He's a curious man, Bernard. *(**VAL** lays down the Canadian Tire bag on the floor.)* I'm sure if he were the head of a military dictatorship, he'd shoot people for dancing. He hates dancing. But on your birthday, Bernard always does

AN EVENING WITH UNCLE VAL • 161

something he hates for you. That's his idea of love. *(Whispers—knowing he is going too far:)* Hate…is his idea of love. *(His good and bad angels argue quietly:)* Now Val! All right. All right.

Bernard is one of what I call the "new townies." They're a queer lot. They got them twangy accents and the Florida tans and they're always laughing a bit too heartily and you can always see the dollar signs in their little crinkly close-set eyes. And if you're from an outport, they're right in love with you—for about fifteen minutes. Oh yes, you're a real curiosity to 'em—like a piece of old driftwood—they wanna squeeeeze the quaintness out of you like a lemon. Personally I prefer the old days when the townie-bayman conflict was out in the open and you could punch someone like Bernard in the nose in a barroom scuffle.

Celia took me out for lunch fer me birthday. She drove. Oh my. She's got one of them special "Zen licences" for the legally blind. We went to one of them new restaurants downtown where we had "medallions" of veal, hand-churned butter, and other dishes "lovingly prepared by the expert staff" for our enjoyment.

As I left the restaurant, I tried to catch a glimpse of the country maidens stationed at their butter churns, but my old eyes are so bad, all I could see was a crowd of cooks in hairnets, desperate to get it all over with and move on to the nearest disco. All very kind people though, especially "Hi, I'm Richard, your waiter. Don't hesitate to call me for any little thing."

My, Jack, we've come a long way here in St. John's, what? What with muffin shops, wicker outlets, and home brew *stores. (Laughing at the idea that anyone would need a store as a source of home brew.)* They seen us coming, Jack. They were waiting at the bottom of the gangplank with trays of doughnuts.

And why didn't they mention them doughnuts before? I'm sure we would have joined Confederation in 1867 if we'd known what an important part doughnuts would play in the cultural fabric. For a while there it looked like the St. John's economy was based on picture framing and hairdressing, but now it's definitely doughnuts.

And from what I hear, the rest of the country is similarly endowed. This is the dough that binds us, the Tim Hortons of Being Earnest, the glaze on the Canadian Shield. *(Pause, then upbeat:)*

I left the restaurant with doggie bags for the poodles, as I found the medallions just a bit too bronzy, then I went home and I had me birthday cake with all seventy-five candles on it, Bernard got drunk, then he got jolly, then he got nasty, then he went to bed.

Margaret come downstairs and we had a few double rums together and one of our very rare chats—which quickly turned to our abiding reminiscence: that of her dear departed mother, Louise, my own true love, God rest her soul. We had a little cry and a little laugh, then a slightly bigger cry, then a slightly bigger glass of rum. Then Margaret toddled off to bed. Well, she didn't *toddle* I suppose but I was just blind and drunk enough to recall that particular memory of her. *(Indicating acid indigestion area of his chest:)* Then I was thinkin' of callin' up "Hi I'm Richard"—see if he'd come by and give me something to settle my stomach. (But I suppose he probably meant "don't hesitate to call" during working hours. Besides, I'd probably never get through to the disco.)

And that was me birthday. A typical exciting day here in the suburbs. I tell you, Jack, I am *truly* blessed. I sit here now surrounded by the electric dishwasher, the cable TV, three hyperactive grandchildren, a successful son-in-law (also hyperactive), a front lawn and two poodles. My socks are washed for me—and dried with Bounce—I have twelve never-worn woollen cardigans still in their Christmas wrap, and daughter Margaret continues to shine with filial devotion. With the exception of my fragile vision, no king could ask for more.

In fact, I just got back from the Canadian Tire. I figured I better spend the gift certificate before Bernard put a stop payment on it. *(Takes a tool belt out of the Canadian Tire bag and straps it on)* I got this groovy new tool belt...wish you could see it. *(Takes an electric drill out of beef bucket, holds it up like a gun)* That's it from here. That's all the news that's fit to print. So long, Jack, *(he guns the drill)* have a nice day *(he guns the drill a few more times)*...and don't hesitate to call me for "any little thing."

As a recording of Sandy Morris's Land and Sea *theme plays,* **VAL** *goes behind the doll's house and begins to drill somewhere at the back of it. He carefully removes a couple of screws and puts them in his pocket.*

TOOL TIME FOR DANES

As the Land and Sea *music continues, he becomes lost in the repair work on the doll's house. He is transformed into the carpenter-host of a Mr. Fixit–style TV show. He looks up from his repair work on the doll's house, as if surprised that there is an audience watching. Music fades. He tells the audience a quick joke in a fake foreign language.*

ANDY: *(The set-up:)* Ah, oh…Valkommen. Meltkniken haben deesn krank melt doosen zu fluct versooken ben oot zut?

(The punch line:) En, to, tre, fire, fem! *(There is canned laughter.* **ANDY** *laughs a bit too heartily and looks to the foreign audience while they are laughing at his joke.)*

Valkommen till Danska Verktygs Showen! *(He is still very amused at his own joke.)*

(Drops his funny-host persona and turns to the real audience.) Sorry, I was just talking to the Danish audience. You probably don't know this, but I've got my own TV show in Denmark; it's called *Tool Time for Danes*. I was just telling the Danes there that there's a lot more to the Uncle Val story. Of course, we couldn't fit it all into one show. One subplot I really miss is the story of Bernard and Margaret's pub on George Street.

Val is the one who *names* the pub. Bernard wanted to call it after a piece of fishing gear that hadn't been used in the name of a bar in St. John's yet. Difficult, but Val comes up with the name: the Grapnel. The bar does well for a while and Val does end up working there. He swore he wouldn't, but he does—he ends up "slingin' beer for Bernard," as he says. And Val turns out to be a bit of a draw. His quaint presence brings in a certain clientele. People like to drop in and hear his stories. But about a year or so into it, just before Christmas of 1989, things turn a little sour. Barely two weeks after Margaret first whispers that there might be *some* financial difficulty, comes Historic Breakfast #1.

164 • ACTOR NEEDS RESTRAINT!

THERE'S A TAVERN IN DISTRESS, BY UNCLE VAL

VAL: *(Walks towards chrome table, stops, looks towards audience.)* And you thought changes come fast in the East Bloc Countries? Oh my, oh my, oh my. My sonny boy, you should be here at 26 Glam Crescent these days. Change? Change? Oh, that Czechoslovakian playwright couldn't be any more shocked than we are.

It all came out during three Historic Breakfasts:

(He sits stage left on the kitchen chair that faces the audience. He lays the drill on the table.) Breakfast #1: There we are, munching toast, cheerfully oblivious that the brooding Bernard has foundation-shaking news to report. Margaret casually inquires how things are. **(VAL** *suddenly stands.)*

"Generally, or specifically?" Bernard demands, suddenly rearing up and snapping out of brood mode and into domestic sabre-rattling. Children go quiet, little mouths wide open, toast and egg on display.

"What difference does it make?" asks Margaret cautiously, barely masking the rising panic in her voice.

"Oh, not very much," *(crossing feet, leaning on table casually)* says Bernard— going for nonchalant now, so as to defuse the steely gaze of worried children. I keep my eyes on my plate, slowly cutting and re-cutting the same piece of egg *(he mimes minimal egg-cutting action)*, afraid that any sudden movement might tip us all into the void. We all know that bad news is imminent. Bernard's eyes begin to dart around the room, looking for escape. But suddenly, he catches sight of all five sets of our eyes. There is no escape. He pauses, panics, then coughs out the word "bankrupt."

Three days later comes Historic Breakfast #2. **(VAL** *walks to the upstage side of the kitchen table and, as his story unfolds, points to where each person in his narrative is sitting.)*

All hands eating porridge in worried silence. Dead quiet. The sound of spoon slicing into porridge is audible. It is obvious that Bernard and Margaret have *another* announcement. What could it be? Bernard starts but begins to cough and mumble at the same time. Margaret takes over. Her mouth is speaking to the children. It is cheery…and false. Her eyes speak to me. They are real and panicky. "We're going to be moving to a new house," she says cheerily.

Jimmy, Kimmy, Bradley, and I exchange glances. Our eyes say, "Oh, my God. The house is gone, too." (**VAL** *walks behind the doll's house as he says:*)

And Historic Breakfast #3 came this morning. Today's announcement: We are moving now. (**VAL** *gets a large cardboard storage box, places it behind the doll's house.*) This is not some vague, futuristic plan. We'll be out of Glam Crescent in a matter of weeks. (*He picks up the roof of the doll's house and places it in the storage box.*)

In the midst of it all, I can only wonder if I am to be sent to an old age home. (*He picks up the main interior structure of the doll's house. It folds in the centre, allowing it to fit neatly on top of the roof in the box.*)

And considering the domino effect in Eastern Europe these days (*he picks up the front exterior of doll's house and puts it in the box*), any change, no matter how drastic, may be just around the corner.

Perhaps this is a soap opera, and my character just isn't getting the ratings. Am I to be written out? (*Picks up the base of the doll's house and puts it in the storage box.*)

Or maybe it was just a bad dream that Bernard had in the shower. (**VAL** *takes off his tool belt and drops it into the box on top of the now collapsed doll's house. He closes the box.*)

How many bedrooms in the new house, I wonder? No one is saying.

Without a pause, **ANDY** *launches into the continuation of the JFK/ Marilyn Monroe story. The lights cross-fade into the dressing room lighting.*

PARLIAMENT OF CULTURAL ROMANCE: THE POLITICS OF FISH

ANDY: (*Walking into dressing room light:*) Then Marilyn Monroe reaches behind her back, takes out a dish towel and holds it out for Kennedy, and says:

MARILYN MONROE: *(Holding out a dish towel)* Someone has some dishes to do.

ANDY: And then Kennedy says:

JFK: Andy, I'm in purgatory. Yeah, I have to wash dishes for a billion years.

ANDY: He takes the dish towel from Marilyn, and I say: "Ah ha! So, there *is* a purgatory?" and he says:

JFK: No. No, you forget you're imagining all this stuff. As far as I know I'm a dusty corpse and that's it.

ANDY: But what about Newfoundland? What do you think about the Parliament of Cultural Romance? Are we a people? And we are just in the middle of some cultural war? And the fittest will survive. Is Anita Best our Winston Churchill? *(With Churchill's rhythms:)* She will fight them on the stage heads. She will never surrender.

Or are we a nation? Fighting for our very life. Is Danny Williams our Churchill? Will he bend our little country to the cause of getting the fish back? Will he never surrender?

But JFK is fading now. He says:

JFK: *(Fading)* The answer's inside your hearts. Because I don't exist. But maybe you should take all that oil money, round up *all* the interested parties in the world, and sit them down in Newfoundland and Labrador. And figure out how to get the fish back! All of the fish—all over the world. *(Kennedy stands on the soapbox/throne and speaks in his "Ask not" inauguration voice:)* Let ah, Newfoundland and Labrador become the United Nations of fish. So, on that sad day when we abandon the oil, we can drown our sorrows in salt and vinegar. On the beautiful and plentiful cold-water purity and deliciousness of cod. Cod! Back again by the basketsful. Worth every penny of your oil profits.

AN EVENING WITH UNCLE VAL • 167

ANDY: *(Still standing on the soapbox, looking upstage towards the vanishing Kennedy and Monroe, and raising his voice:)* Then I say, "But if I'm generating all this stuff in my own brain, how can I trust it?!" And Marilyn Monroe speaks to me—but Uncle Val's voice comes out.

VAL/FRANCIS COLBERT/MARILYN MONROE: *(In a Job's Cove accent)* I dunno. Just relax, Andy. You can't know. You're still in the middle of it. I gotta say, you're not bad like Vince yourself—hanging around with the *Kennedys*. But I s'pose that's just "cubist theatre," is it?

This is Francis Colbert, by the way, not Uncle Val. But I s'pose you think if you've seen one senior citizen you've seen 'em all. All. All. All. *(He does the fading-echo voice as he steps off the soapbox and moves to the area downstage of the kitchen table.)*

ANDY: Make no mistake about it, the aims of the Parliament of Cultural Romance were political. We were the first generation of Newfoundland and Labrador Canadians, and our generation figured it was our job to spark the debate that would galvanize "our story of ourselves" in order that we might eventually take our place at the adults' table of Canada, to eventually become a "have" province, a homeland that our children could stay in, proud of this gem of a culture that we had brought with us into Confederation.

At least that's what I thought we were trying to do, and, of course, I hoped Uncle Val would be a part of that. I can only speak for that somewhat sensitive middle-class young fellow worrying about the fishery and the potholes on Portugal Cove Road.

But then *(sits on soapbox/throne at centre stage)*, five years after that great wedding feast, I was one of a group of actors who dramatized one of his stories and brought it back to Mr. Pius Power Sr. We took the coastal boat down Placentia Bay all the way to South East Bight. There are no roads there, so we had to carry all the equipment and the props and costumes on our shoulders, on our backs, over the barrens, over the marshes and the meadows—up to the new school gymnasium, where we performed *Jack Meets the Cat*, a story which Mr. Power had told to his family and friends in his own kitchen. And, though there was some Disneyfication and reworking of plot, the play was filled with his humour and wit and turn of phrase.

It was like *we* were Jack now. We'd gone down the road, had lots of adventures, and we'd made it back home again—with stories to tell!

And Mr. Power really liked it.

Later in the evening, there was a dance at the school gymnasium, and we were invited down (**ANDY** *stands and walks downstage*), and a bunch of us stood in the middle of the dance floor with Mr. Power—with people dancing and spinning all around us—and he told us a story I'd never heard. The story was called "Jack Shits in the Gentleman's Shoes." I was in heaven!

Maybe I *am* a romantic middle-class townie…maybe…but that place (this place) made me, guaranteed. And somehow gave me that extraordinary, infectious, and probably foolish—and maybe totally hopeless— yet ever-regenerating passion that we all still seem to have for Newfoundland and Labrador.

I wonder how the young people think we have done so far. I guess I'll have to telephone Alberta to find out.

FAREWELL TO COZY CUL-DE-SACS, BY UNCLE VAL

ANDY *reverts quickly to being* **UNCLE VAL**; *he stands and speaks directly to the audience.*

VAL: January 6th, 1990. Old Christmas Day.

Dear Jack, Sorry we haven't done the Christmas thing. A state of flux here, actually. Since my last letter, the bankruptcy has untimely ripped us from the suburban comfort of Glam Crescent, and we have been deposited on the serious fringes of the downtown. So serious that I can see the harbour water out my bedroom window.

I'm lucky to be here at all, as I came dangerously close to walking the plank for a couple of days there, while Margaret talked about "early admission" at a local seniors' establishment. But I boldly pointed out that my old age pension, my savings, and undeniable babysitting skills would be too great a loss.

So here I am, available for the round-table post-mortems, the analysis of how it all went wrong.

Margaret has arranged counselling, and believe it or not, we, as a family, are sitting down and talking. Well, that might be a bit of an exaggeration, but we have *begun* to move *towards* talking *around* the general area that we really wish to discuss. But this is a step forward. After all, the family did arrive here in the late 1700s, and it really was about time somebody sat down and talked. *(Sits on the doll's house box by the kitchen table.)*

Anyway, now here we are in old St. John's, where rum is not all that cheap; here with little winding streets, the back alleys, narrow clapboard, corner stores, and dog population only equalled by that of Mexico City. That is, until Bernard schemes us all back up the social ladder again. Yes, surely this is an interlude, a limbo, a holding tank. We are in a play, and our real life in the suburbs awaits us. In the next scene, I walk over to the stage right window *(getting carried away, he walks to extreme downstage right)* and stare out at the South Side Hills, hoping they will give me some sort of answer. But then, dramatically *(returns dramatically to centre stage),* I turn to *(on his left:)* Jimmy and Kimmy, *(on his right:)* Bradley and the poodles, and say, *(sounding more like Francis Colbert at his most passionate:)* they are just hills! Silent wintry mounds—not some message of doom telegraphed from your future! So, youth of Newfoundland and youth of Labrador, FEAR NOT!

Jimmy, Kimmy, Bradley, the poodles, the goldfish, the gerbil, and Bernard and Margaret, who have just entered stage left, all burst into applause. The audience joins in. The curtain falls, we are all whisked out of the theatre to our limousine and back to the suburbs!

(Walking towards the doll's house stand:) But in the meantime I'd better get to know the neighbours, just in case. *(Sitting on the toy box:)* I'm after meetin' a whole yaffle of people just from my daily walk with Bradley from the bubble in the harbour up to Bannerman Park, over to Rawlins Cross and down to the old Longshoremen's Protective Union Hall on Victoria Street. Yeah, the LSPU. *(Peers investigatively at the audience.)* Now,

they look like an interesting crowd. Oh yeah, I'd say there's lots more stories to tell and lots more storytellers to tell 'em.

As they say in the movies, "To be continued."

As the final lights fade, we hear the pre-recorded music of Duane Andrews playing the "Portuguese Waltzes."

Blackout.

An Evening with Uncle Val was first presented at the LSPU Hall, St. John's, Newfoundland and Labrador from November 21–24 and December 1–3, 2006.

The show was dedicated to the memory of the various voices of Val, especially Francis Colbert, Michael Jones Sr., Pius Power Sr., Pius Power Jr., and Ab Stockwood.

Performed by **ANDY JONES**
Direction and dramaturgy by **LOIS BROWN**
Script written by **ANDY JONES** with **MICHAEL JONES SR.**
Sound design by **HARVEY HYSLOP**
Lighting design by **ROBERT GAUTHIER**
Stage technicians: **ROBERT GAUTHIER** and **PAT DEMPSEY**
Backstage crew: **STEPHEN DUNN** and **DIANA JONES**
Pre-recorded music: "While Shepherds Watched Their Flocks by
   Night" (Green's Harbour version) sung by **ELLEN POWER**;
   "Portuguese Waltzes" played by **DUANE ANDREWS**; *Land and
   Sea* theme ("On the Beach") performed by **SANDY MORRIS**;
   Jazz Suite No. 2 Waltz No. 2, by **DMITRI SHOSTAKOVICH**
Set: **LOIS BROWN** and **MARY-LYNN BERNARD**, with
   OLIVIA CURTIS BROWN and **RUTH LAWRENCE**

Set reinforcement by **JEFF BAGGS**
Shea Street doll's house design and construction: **JEFF BAGGS**
Shea Street doll's house interior/exterior painting: **HEATHER READ**
Costumes: **MARY-LYNN BERNARD**
Props: **MARY-LYNN BERNARD**
"Tiffy" and Spider-Man cape: **PEGGY HOGAN**
"Tuffy": **MARY-LYNN BERNARD**
Poster concept: **JANET RUSSELL**
Poster design: **JOHN ANDREWS** and **MIKE MOULAND**
House on Shea Street photo: **PAUL DALY**
Publicity coordination: **CHERIE PYNE**
Additional publicity: **RHONDA BUCKLEY**
Production assistants: **MARY-LYNN BERNARD, ERIN
    FRENCH, NICOLE ROUSSEAU, LUKE MAJOR**
Company administration: **CHERIE PYNE**

Thanks for additional script from my father, Michael Jones Sr.—from our many conversations about aging and particularly for his scripted material, which was eventually broadcast in his own "Memoirs of a Hospital Survivor," produced by Glen Tilley of CBC St. John's.

And thanks for anecdotes and inspiration from Mary-Lynn Bernard, Mary Walsh, Mary (Dalton) Walsh (who first wondered where all the fairies had disappeared to), Bill Cooper (for his colicky baby stories), and Ella Scott (who owns "Val's house" on Shea Street).

For inspiration regarding Val's neighbour Vince, I'd like to thank my mother, Agnes (Dobbin) Jones, who had recurring dreams of a close personal friendship with Queen Elizabeth; Wilson Warren, who reported a real friendship with the queen throughout his time in Scotland during the Second World War; and the recitation "Sam's Sturgeon," by Ashley Sterne (1935).

Thanks to Marnie Parsons and Janet Russell for collecting and transcribing the letters of Uncle Val, thus launching this whole production. Thanks to Janet Russell for producing the CD *The Letters of Uncle Val* on the Rattling Books label (available online).

Thanks to Anita Best and the late Pius Power Jr. and their respective families for their endlessly inspiring wedding.

Also, sincere thanks to the CBC "Uncle Val Angels," including Arthur Black (of *Basic Black*), Bill Squires, Glen Tilley, John Disney, John Doyle, John Spittal, and John Foster—Uncle Val was born on CBC Radio!

And special thanks to Victor Tilley, Jason Smith, Shannon Hawes, Geoff Younghusband, Dini Conte, Dr. Chesley Brown, Sheila's Brush Theatre Company, Connie Corkum Hynes, Gerry Rogers, Dog Meat BBQ, Jim Rillie, Chris Brookes, Sandy Morris, Mark Ferguson, the Newfoundland and Labrador Archives, Shauna McCabe of the Provincial Art Gallery, Ruth "the serendipitous" Canning, Marthe Bernard, Louis Bernard, Gord Taylor, Olivia Curtis Brown, Rhonda and Emma Taylor, Marian Optical, Mack Furlong, Doug Colbert, Larry Dohey, the staff of the LSPU Hall, the Newfoundland and Labrador Arts Council, the City of St. John's Arts Jury, and the Cultural Economic Development Program of the Government of Newfoundland and Labrador's Tourism, Culture and Recreation Department.

I left a number of things in the script that I know Uncle Val got wrong. For example, he thinks that "Scarios" were made by Chef Boyardee and that Haystack Calhoun created the "coco bonk." In fact, Heinz Foods made "Scarios," and apparently what Haystack Calhoun invented was called the "coco butt."

This version of *An Evening with Uncle Val* was based on performances at Theatre Passe Muraille, Toronto, Ontario, from September 30 to October 18, 2008.

TOURING HISTORY

An Evening with Uncle Val was first presented at the LSPU Hall, St. John's, Newfoundland and Labrador, from November 21–24 and December 1–3, 2006.

In 2007, coordinated by Nicole Rousseau and stage managed by Geoff Younghusband, *Uncle Val* played at On the Waterfront Festival, Alderney Landing Theatre, in Halifax, Nova Scotia, from May 4 to 6.

In November of 2007, *Uncle Val* toured eight Arts and Culture Centres across Newfoundland and Labrador: Corner Brook, Stephenville, Grand Falls–Windsor, Gander, St. John's, Carbonear, Goose Bay, and Labrador West.

An Evening with Uncle Val was included in Toronto's Theatre Passe Muraille's 2008 season and played a three-week run there from September 30 to October 18.

From 2008 to 2010 Andy toured *Uncle Val* nationally: January 9 and 10, 2008, at One Yellow Rabbit's High Performance Rodeo, Calgary,

Alberta; January 12 at the West End Cultural Centre, Winnipeg, Manitoba; and January 19 at the Margaret Greenham Theatre, Banff Centre, Banff, Alberta. Other presentations include February 7 and 8 at Market Hall, Peterborough, Ontario; February 9 at the Richmond Hill Centre for the Performing Arts in association with the Curtain Club, Richmond Hill, Toronto; the Uno Festival, Victoria, British Columbia; Presentation House Theatre with Intrepid Theatre, Vancouver, British Columbia; and Magnetic North Theatre Festival, Ottawa, Ontario.

From July 17 to August 10, 2008, *Uncle Val* toured the Maritimes, including the Al Whittle Theatre, Wolfville, Nova Scotia; Mulgrave Road Theatre at the Chedabucto Place Performance Centre, Guysborough, Nova Scotia; Victoria Playhouse, Victoria, Prince Edward Island; Ship's Company Theatre, Parrsboro, Nova Scotia; Ocean View Theatre, Rocky Harbour, Newfoundland and Labrador; and the Warehouse Theatre, Cow Head, Newfoundland and Labrador.

From February 20 to March 1, 2009, *Uncle Val* toured Ontario, including Oakville Centre for the Performing Arts, Oakville; Gryphon Theatre, Barrie; Royal Bank Theatre, Mississauga; Kingston Grand Theatre, Kingston; Rose Theatre, Brampton; and Markham Theatre, Markham.

From March 31 to April 5, 2009, Sunshine Theatre presented *Uncle Val* at the Rotary Centre for the Arts, Kelowna, British Columbia. From November 3 to 8, 2009, it played at the Surrey Arts Centre in Surrey, British Columbia.

Other performances that year included Point Leamington Academy, Point Leamington, Newfoundland and Labrador; the Pivot Festival, Whitehorse, Northwest Territories; Confederation Centre's Studio 2, Charlottetown, Prince Edward Island; Imperial Theatre, Saint John, New Brunswick; Riverview Arts Centre, Riverview, New Brunswick; Osprey Arts Centre, Shelburne, Nova Scotia; and the Astor Theatre, Liverpool, Nova Scotia (with Contact East).

In 2011 *An Evening with Uncle Val* played from March 3–14 in the Fringe Theatre Adventures, Edmonton, Alberta.

PRODUCTION NOTES

There were a number of versions of this show. The version herein is based on the original production at the LSPU Hall in November of 2006 and the Theatre Passe Muraille 2008 version.

Sketches came and went during the life of this show. Some were new; some were recycled from Andy Jones's previous one-man shows. The Uncle Val letters, the personal reminiscences, the Kennedys, and "The Parliament of Cultural Romance" were, however, in all versions.

Props, Costumes, and Set Pieces

Costumes, Part One: Uncle Val's white shirt, blue suit pants, blue suit jacket, blue tie, black socks, black shoes.

Costumes, Part Two: Actor's street clothes, including black pants, shoes, red shirt, black T-shirt, and black socks.

Costumes that are pre-set as props: winter coat, salt-and-pepper hat, Christmas stocking that becomes a jester's hat, poodle slippers, cardigan, starter pistol in pocket at top of show, pen in shirt pocket, brand new tool belt, and fox-fur cloak with stuffed toy dog attached.

Props and set pieces: large cardboard boxes; Uncle Val's writing table; lamp on writing table with cord going offstage; writing table chair; area rug for under Uncle Val's writing desk; snow device rigged in grid with release string hanging down to the stage level; doll's house (facing audience for top of Part One and Part Two); large cardboard storage box for dismantled doll's house; tiny device for snow inside the doll's house (for Part One); chrome kitchen table stage left; metal garbage bin; matching chair for chrome kitchen table; movable Canada Post mailbox on prop stick; newspapers flowing out of some boxes; coat tree stage right; coloured blanket on middle chair/ box; one box in the way stage right of doll's house (set at top of Part One only); music box; middle box/chair/throne; wooden writing secretary (if possible); fox-fur coat; Canadian

Tire shopping bag; electric drill; new tool belt; writing paper; envelopes; stamps; pens; starter pistol; starter pistol blanks; used diaper (folded); Uncle Val's cozy blanket (Part Two) (light blue); practical working kettle; practical extension cord for kettle; Idahoan brand potato flakes (for snow); moving boxes; moving blankets; Christmas decorations; Christmas tree (for Christmas version of show only); Christmas crèche with tiny dolls representing Bernard, Margaret, baby Jesus, Jimmy, Kimmy, the poodles, and Uncle Val; a child's Spider-Man cape; a cardboard box with plastic crown; children's toys; a teapot; a sugar bowl with a cover and sugar; a teaspoon; two cups; reading glasses on the table; power drill, power drill screw bit in place; beef bucket (with power drill in it); poodle slippers; upholsterer's black thread (to pull poodles off stage); plastic bag to hold tool belt; baby's Christmas rattle; cardboard divider/glass protectors to be used as a human brain; a Carnation milk can with holes for pouring (check each night to see they are not blocked), and empty cardboard Carnation milk box, Tetley tea bags in the box, and Purity Lemon Creams.

For a long time scientists believed that overacting was viral, was passed on—actor to actor—from a sneeze, a kiss or from wearing the costume of someone who previously overacted in the same role. But now! Scientists working on the great genome project believe that they have isolated the "overacting gene", that overacting may run in families, that only by sterilizing certain actors might we wipe this plague out forever. But hang on—"that's a little extreme" you might think. Well, so do a lot of actors whose close work with scientists has led to the discovery of acting gaskets in the human brain which seal in various human brain liquids and which if overtaxed can be dislodged—yes, that's right, it's possible to "blow an acting gasket."

Short bursts of overacting can be therapeutic. They contain the seeds of their own cure: an explosive release which serves to calm the actor.

but, 2.

*PROLONGED OVERACTING can lead to...

Muscles which haven't been used in awhile actually twitch

But here we see prolonged overacting. Every muscle in the body is tense; even some muscles which have never been used before are twitching, which can lead to blowing an acting gasket and then a buildup of hot brain liquids which might burst the side of the skull, as we see in the next picture.

Many older actors and some younger ones who seem to have had a stroke or who shout incoherently at the audience or wander aimlessly about the stage with insane rolling eyes may be the innocent victims of a blown acting gasket. Pharmaceutical labs throughout the country are rushing to find a medication to control, but unfortunately never to cure, this deadly genetic discovery.

This looks a bit like Elmo from Sesame Street. Elmo with hot brain liquids bursting out of his head, could be the big thing next Christmas...

ACKNOWLEDGEMENTS

Thank you to Charlie Tomlinson, who helped me with every aspect of this book, and to kind readers Don McKay, Rachel Dragland, and Lois Brown.

Thank you for your backing and support to Rebecca Rose, Rhonda Molloy, and all the crew at Breakwater, and for administrative assistance to Jenny Naish and Walter Ferguson-O'Brien.

To Mary-Lynn Bernard, Marthe Jones Bernard, Mary Win Clair, Mark Ferguson, and Brenda O'Brien—thanks for keeping me going.

And very special thanks to Claire Wilkshire for her trenchant editing, her kind and encouraging words, and her patient and wonderful suggestions.

ANDY JONES has been a professional writer and actor for over forty years. He has written five critically acclaimed one-man comedy shows. He is well-known as one of the members of the groundbreaking Newfoundland comedy troupe CODCO, in both its theatrical and television incarnations, and as a writer for CBC's *Kids in the Hall* series. He has written six children's books rooted in Newfoundland folk culture. Andy's numerous accolades include two Gemini awards, election to the Newfoundland and Labrador Arts Council Hall of Honour, the BMO Winterset Award, Best Performance at the Atlantic Film Festival in Halifax, and the ACTRA Award of Excellence for Lifetime Achievement.